First World War
and Army of Occupation
War Diary
France, Belgium and Germany

20 DIVISION
Divisional Troops
Divisional Ammunition Column
28 July 1915 - 21 April 1919

WO95/2106/3

The Naval & Military Press Ltd
www.nmarchive.com
Published in association with The National Archives

Published by

The Naval & Military Press Ltd

Unit 10 Ridgewood Industrial Park,

Uckfield, East Sussex,

TN22 5QE England

Tel: +44 (0) 1825 749494

www.naval-military-press.com

www.nmarchive.com

This diary has been reprinted in facsimile from the original. Any imperfections are inevitably reproduced and the quality may fall short of modern type and cartographic standards.

© **Crown Copyright**
Images reproduced by permission of The National Archives, London, England, 2015.

Contents

Document type	Place/Title	Date From	Date To
Heading	2106/3		
Heading	20th Division Divl Artillery 20th Divl Ammn Col Jly 1915-Apl 1919		
Heading	20th Division 20th Divn. O.C. Vol I July To August 15		
War Diary	Au Souverain	01/08/1915	01/08/1915
War Diary	Commune Of Hazebrouck	01/08/1915	01/08/1915
War Diary	Affringues	28/07/1915	28/07/1915
War Diary	Arques	28/07/1915	28/07/1915
War Diary	Au Souverain	29/07/1915	31/07/1915
Heading	20th Divl. Ammunition Column Vol II		
War Diary	Au Souverain	02/08/1915	28/08/1915
War Diary	Estaires	30/08/1915	30/08/1915
War Diary	Au Souverain	09/08/1915	09/08/1915
Heading	20th Divl A.C. Vol 3 Sept & Oct 15		
Miscellaneous	Officer i/c R.A. Sector. A.G.S.	02/11/1915	02/11/1915
War Diary	Ref Sheet 36a L 22c. 7.7	04/09/1915	26/09/1915
War Diary	L.22.c.7.7	27/09/1915	30/10/1915
Heading	20th D.A.C. Vol 4 Nov 15		
War Diary	L.22.c.7.7 Sheet 36A	01/11/1915	30/11/1915
Heading	20th D.A.C. Vol 5		
War Diary	L.22.c.7.7 Sheet 36a.	01/12/1915	31/12/1915
Heading	20th D.A.C. Vol 6		
War Diary	L.22.c.7.7 Sheet 36a.	01/01/1916	10/01/1916
War Diary	Estaires	11/01/1916	22/01/1916
War Diary	Hazebrouck	23/01/1916	23/01/1916
War Diary	Lederzeele	24/01/1916	31/01/1916
Heading	20th D.A.C. Vol 7		
War Diary	Lederzeele	01/02/1916	03/02/1916
War Diary	Arneke	04/02/1916	14/02/1916
War Diary	A.18.c.6.2 (Sheet 28)	14/02/1916	14/02/1916
War Diary	Hamhoek	14/02/1916	04/04/1916
War Diary	Poperinghe	04/04/1916	17/04/1916
War Diary	Hamhoek	18/04/1916	19/04/1916
War Diary	Bollezeele	19/04/1916	19/04/1916
War Diary	Rubrouck	20/04/1916	20/04/1916
War Diary	Rubrouck	18/04/1916	19/04/1916
War Diary	Rubrouck	25/04/1916	30/04/1916
War Diary	Rubrouck Sheet 27	05/05/1916	15/05/1916
War Diary	Rubrouck	12/05/1916	20/05/1916
War Diary	Peselhoek Poperinghe Sheet 28	21/05/1916	31/05/1916
War Diary	Peselhoek	31/05/1916	30/06/1916
Heading	War Diary Divisional Ammunition Column, 20th Division. July 1916		
War Diary	Peselhoek And Vlamatinghe	01/07/1916	29/07/1916
Heading	20th Division Artillery. 20th Divisional Ammunition Column August 1916		
Heading	War Diary 20th Divl D.A.C. 5th To 31st August 1916 (Volume XIV)		
Miscellaneous	Staff Captain R.A. 20th Division	31/08/1916	31/08/1916
War Diary	Peselhoek and Vlamatinghe	05/08/1916	30/08/1916

War Diary	Couin	01/08/1916	16/08/1916
War Diary	Beauval	17/08/1916	17/08/1916
War Diary	Boisbergues	18/08/1916	18/08/1916
War Diary	Havernas	19/08/1916	19/08/1916
War Diary	Vacquemont	20/08/1916	20/08/1916
War Diary	Near Meaulte	22/08/1916	31/08/1916
Heading	20th Divisional Artillery. 20th Divisional Ammunition Column September 1916		
Heading	War Diary 20th Divl Ammn Coln From Sep 1st 1916 To Sept 30th 1916 Vol		
War Diary	Peselhoek	01/09/1916	08/09/1916
War Diary	Zermezeele	08/09/1916	09/09/1916
War Diary	Rebecq	09/09/1916	10/09/1916
War Diary	EPS	10/09/1916	11/09/1916
War Diary	Monchel	11/09/1916	12/09/1916
War Diary	La Maillard	12/09/1916	13/09/1916
War Diary	Naours	13/09/1916	14/09/1916
War Diary	Bois Des Tailles	14/09/1916	29/09/1916
War Diary	Carnoy	30/09/1916	30/09/1916
Heading	20th Divisional Artillery. 20th Divisional Ammunition Column October 1916		
Heading	War Diary Of 20th Divisional Ammunition Column R.F.A. From 1st October 1916 to 31st October 1916		
Miscellaneous	Staff Captain R.A. 20th Division	31/10/1916	31/10/1916
War Diary	Carnoy	01/10/1916	31/10/1916
Heading	20th Divisional Artillery 20th Divisional Ammunition Column November 1916		
Heading	War Diary For Nov 1st to 30th 1916 20th Divisional Ammunition Column		
Miscellaneous	Bde Major R.A. 20th Division	20/11/1916	20/11/1916
War Diary	Carnoy	01/11/1916	29/11/1916
War Diary	Carnoy	22/11/1916	26/11/1916
Heading	20th Divisional Artillery 20th Divisional Ammunition Column December 1916		
Heading	War Diary December 1916 (Original Copy)		
War Diary	F.17.d.9.9 Albert Combiend Sheet	01/12/1916	27/12/1916
Heading	War Diary 20th Divisional Ammunition Column R.F.A. January 1917 Vol 18		
War Diary	F.17.d.9.9 (Albert Combiend Sheet)	02/01/1917	29/01/1917
Heading	War Diary 20th Div. Ammun. Col. Vol 19		
War Diary	F 17 D 9.9 (Albert Combiend Sheet)	03/02/1917	27/02/1917
Heading	War Diary 20th Divnl Ammtn. Column March 1917 Vol 20		
War Diary		01/03/1917	27/03/1917
Heading	War Diary of 20th Divnl. Ammtn. Column R.F.A. From 1st April 1917 to 30th April 1917 Vol 21		
War Diary	Leuze Wood Map of France Sheet 57c 1/40000	01/04/1917	08/04/1917
War Diary	Leuze Wood	08/04/1917	17/04/1917
War Diary	Bus	18/04/1917	28/04/1917
Heading	War Diary of 1st May 1917 to 31st May 1917 20th Div. Ammn Coln Vol 22		
War Diary	Bus	01/05/1917	21/05/1917
War Diary	Bus	20/04/1917	31/05/1917
Heading	War Diary 20th Divisional Ammunition Column From 1st June to 30th June 1917 Vol 23		
Miscellaneous	Cover for Documents. Nature of Enclosures.		

War Diary	Camp Near Favreuil Map of France Sheet 57c. Map of France H 22 B	01/06/1917	30/06/1917
Heading	War Diary Of 20th Div. Ammun. Col. 1st to 31st July 1917 (Vol 7)		
War Diary	In The Field Map Lens 11.	03/07/1917	07/07/1917
War Diary	In The Field Map Hazebrouck 5A	08/07/1917	12/07/1917
War Diary	Map Of Belgium and France Sheet 28 A 14 D8.3	13/07/1917	31/07/1917
Miscellaneous	O.C. Divisional Ammn Col.	26/07/1917	26/07/1917
Miscellaneous	Dear Colonel	30/07/1917	30/07/1917
Miscellaneous	My Dear Foster	29/07/1917	29/07/1917
Miscellaneous	Military Medal		
Heading	War Diary 20th Divl. Ammn Coln R.F.A. 1st-31st August 1917 Vol 25		
War Diary	B 21 B 7.8 (Map of Belgium & France Sheet 28)	01/08/1917	17/08/1917
War Diary	B 21 B 7.8 (Map of Belgium & France Sheet 28)	07/08/1917	31/08/1917
War Diary	Dear Foster	11/08/1917	11/08/1917
Heading	War Diary Of 20th Divisional Ammn. Column. From 1.9.17 To 30.9.17 Volume 9		
Miscellaneous	Cover for Documents. Nature of Enclosures.		
War Diary	Map of Belgium & France Sheet 28 B 13 B 2.8	01/09/1917	15/09/1917
War Diary	Map of Belgium & France Sheet 28 (B 13 B 2.8)	13/09/1917	30/09/1917
Heading	War Diary Of 20th. Divnl. Ammn. Column. From 1st October to 31st October. 1917 Vol 10		
War Diary	Map Of Belgium & France Sheet 28 B 13 B 2.8	01/10/1917	22/10/1917
War Diary	V 28 D 4.4 Sheet 57c.	23/10/1917	30/10/1917
War Diary	V 28 D 4.4 Sheet 57c.	29/10/1917	31/10/1917
Heading	War Diary of 20th Divisional Ammunition Column From 1st Nov. To 30th November 1917 Vol 11		
War Diary	Nurlu (Sheet 62 C D 4 A and B)	01/11/1917	21/11/1917
War Diary	W 13 B Sheet 57c	22/11/1917	26/11/1917
War Diary	Nurlu Sheet 62c D 4. A And B	27/11/1917	30/11/1917
Heading	War Diary of 20th Divisional Ammunition Column From 1st Dec to 31st December 1917 Vol 12		
War Diary	Nurlu (Sheet 57c).	01/12/1917	14/12/1917
War Diary	Line Of March	15/12/1917	31/12/1917
Heading	War Diary Of 20th Divisional Ammunition Column R.F.A. From 1st Jany To 31st Jany 1918 Vol 4		
War Diary	Croix De Poperinghe Square M 32 B Sheet 28	01/01/1918	21/01/1918
War Diary	Zevecoten Square G 35 C Sheet 28	22/01/1918	31/01/1918
Heading	War Diary Of 20th D.A.C. From 1st to 28th February 1918 Vol 31		
Miscellaneous	Cover for Documents. Nature of Enclosures.		
War Diary	(G. 35c) Sheet 28 Map Of Belgium & France	01/02/1918	18/02/1918
War Diary	Line Of March	19/02/1918	28/02/1918
Heading	20th Divisional Artillery. 20th Divisional Ammunition Colum R.F.A. March 1918		
Heading	War Diary of 20th Divl. Ammunition Column From 1st to 31st March 1918 Vol III		
Miscellaneous	Cover for Documents. Nature of Enclosures.		
War Diary		01/03/1918	21/03/1918
War Diary	Line Of March	22/03/1918	24/03/1918
War Diary	Line Of March Map Of Amiens	25/03/1918	31/03/1918
Heading	War Diary Of 20th Divnl. Ammn. Col. 1-4-18 To 30-4-18 Vol 4		
War Diary	Line Of March Map Of Amiens Dieppe & Abbeville	01/04/1918	15/04/1918

War Diary	Line Of March Map Of Amiens Dieppe & Abbeville Sheet 62d Map Of France	16/04/1918	24/04/1918
War Diary	Line Of March Map Of Amiens & Line Of Sheet 62 D	25/04/1918	30/04/1918
War Diary	Rouy Le Petit	21/03/1918	21/03/1918
War Diary	Villers St Christophe	22/03/1918	23/03/1918
War Diary	Rethonvillers	24/03/1918	24/03/1918
War Diary	Cremery	25/03/1918	25/03/1918
War Diary	Le Quesnil	26/03/1918	26/03/1918
War Diary	Villers-Au-Erables	27/03/1918	28/03/1918
War Diary	Sains-En-Amienois	29/03/1918	01/04/1918
War Diary	Quevauvillers	02/04/1918	03/04/1918
War Diary	Namps-Au-Mont	04/04/1918	06/04/1918
War Diary	Quevauvillers	07/04/1918	09/04/1918
War Diary	Brocourt	10/04/1918	10/04/1918
War Diary	Grecourt-Mesnil	11/04/1918	11/04/1918
War Diary	Longroy	12/04/1918	17/04/1918
War Diary	Eaucourt	18/04/1918	18/04/1918
War Diary	Villers L'Hopital	19/04/1918	19/04/1918
War Diary	Merlin-Le-Sec	20/04/1918	20/04/1918
War Diary	Mingoval	21/04/1918	03/05/1918
War Diary	Ablain St Nazaire	04/05/1918	05/05/1918
Miscellaneous	Dear Faster	06/04/1918	06/04/1918
Heading	War Diary Of 20th Divl. Ammn. Column. From 1st To 31st May 1918 Vol V		
Miscellaneous	Cover for Documents. Nature of Enclosures.		
War Diary	Line Of March Map Lens 11	01/05/1918	04/05/1918
War Diary	Gouy-Servins Q 35 D Map Sheet 36 B.	05/05/1918	31/05/1918
Heading	War Diary Of 20th Divl. Ammn. Column From 1st To 30th June 1918 Vol VI		
Miscellaneous	Cover for Documents Nature of Enclosures.		
War Diary	Headquarters No 1 And 2 Section Gouy-Servins (Q35D) Sheet 44 B No 3 Section Ablain-St-Nazaire (XIOA & B)	05/06/1918	29/06/1918
Heading	War Diary Of 20th Divnl. Ammn. Column, From 1st To 31st July 1918 Vol VII		
Miscellaneous	Cover For Documents. Nature Of Enclosures.		
War Diary	Headquarters No 1 And 2 Section Gouy-Servins (Q35D) Sheet 44 B No 3 Section Ablain-St-Nazaire (XIOA & B)	02/07/1918	29/07/1918
Heading	War Diary Of 20th Divl. Ammn. Column From 1st To 31st August 1918 Vol VIII		
Miscellaneous	Cover for Documents. Nature of Enclosures.		
War Diary	Headquarters No 1 And 2 Section Gouy-Servins (Q35D) Sheet 44 B No 3 Section Ablain-St-Nazaire (XIOA & B)	02/08/1918	26/08/1918
Heading	War Diary Of 20th Divl. Ammn. Column. From 1st To 30th Sept 1918 Vol IX		
Miscellaneous	Cover for Documents Nature of Enclosures.		
War Diary	Headquarters No 1 And 2 Section Gouy-Servins (Q35D) Sheet 44 B No 3 Section Ablain-St-Nazaire (XIOA & B)	06/09/1918	29/09/1918
Heading	War Diary Of 20th Divl. Amm. Column From 1st To 31st October 1918 Vol X		
Diagram etc			
Miscellaneous	Cover for Documents. Nature of Enclosures.		

War Diary	HQ. No 1 and 2 Section At Gouy-Servins No 3 Section At Ablain-St-Nazaire Subsequently Line Of March Map France Map Lens 11	01/10/1918	09/10/1918
War Diary	France Camp At Cherisy Vis-En-Artois Road Map France Map Lens 11	10/10/1918	31/10/1918
Heading	War Diary Of 20th Divnl. Ammn. Column. From 1.11.18 To 30.11.18 Vol XI		
Miscellaneous	Cover for Documents. Nature of Enclosures.		
War Diary	March An Cambrai And Line Of March	01/11/1918	06/11/1918
War Diary	Line Of March	07/11/1918	27/11/1918
War Diary	Pommier (Sheet Lens 11)	28/11/1918	30/11/1918
Heading	War Diary Of 20th Divisional Ammn. Col. From 1.12.18 To 31.12.18 Vol 12		
Miscellaneous	Cover For Documents. Nature Of Enclosures.		
War Diary	HQ. No. 1 And 2 Section Pommier No. 3 Section Warlincourt Rifle Sheet Lens 11		
Heading	War Diary Of 20th Divnl. Ammunition Column. From 1st Jan. 1919 To 31st Jan. 1919 Vol I		
Miscellaneous	Cover For Documents. Nature Of Enclosures.		
War Diary	H.Q. No. 1 and 2 Sections Pommier No. 3 Section. Warlincourt Rifle. Sheet Lens. 11		
Heading	War Diary of 20th Divnl Ammunition Col from; 1.2.19. to 28.2.19. Vol. 2		
Miscellaneous	Cover for Documents. Nature of Enclosures.		
War Diary	H.Q. No 1 And 2 Section Pommier No. 3 Section Warlincourt Rifle. Sheet Lens 11	00/02/1919	21/04/1919
Miscellaneous	S.O. 20th Divl. M.T. Coy	04/04/1919	04/04/1919
Heading	20th Division.		
Miscellaneous	O.C. 20 D.A.C.		
Miscellaneous	Dear McGaven		
Miscellaneous	D.O.C. Was Formed About 15th Jany 15 Lt Col R. Foster RHA in Canadian.		
Miscellaneous	D.A.C. 3 Section at beginning		
Miscellaneous	Headquarters Lt. Col. G.R. Foster R.F.A. Mention Oct/16	16/10/1919	16/10/1919
Miscellaneous	No 3 Section	17/10/1919	17/10/1919
Miscellaneous	Officer Of D.A.C. During Companies		
Miscellaneous	20th Divisional Ammunition Column R.F.A. Casualties.		
Miscellaneous			
Miscellaneous	History Of No 1 Section 20th D.A.C.		
Miscellaneous	No 9 20 Div. D.A.C.		
Miscellaneous	History Of No 2 Section 20th Div. Ammn Column R.F.A.		
Miscellaneous	History Of No. 2 Section 20th D.A.G.		
Miscellaneous	History Of 3rd Section 20th D.A.C.		

2106/3

20TH DIVISION
DIVL ARTILLERY

20TH DIVL AMMN COL.
JLY 1915-APL 1919.

20ᵗʰ Division

20ᵗʰ Divis: A.C.
Vol: I

July & August 15. – Sept '19.

CONFIDENTIAL.

WAR DIARY
INTELLIGENCE SUMMARY.
(Erase heading not required.)

Army Form C. 2118

Instructions regarding War Diaries and Intelligence Summaries are contained in F. S. Regs., Part II. and the Staff Manual respectively. Title pages will be prepared in manuscript.

Place	Date	Hour	Summary of Events and Information	Remarks and references to Appendices
AU SOUVERAIN COMMUNE OF HAZEBROUCK	1915 1 Aug.	3.10 p.m.	The 26th Divisional Ammunition Column was formed on 15/7/15 and went into training. JJB	
			The Column left England (Larkhill, Salisbury Plain) for France on the 22/7/15 arriving at HAVRE on the morning of the 24/7/15. departed same day for LUMBRES arriving at 6.30 a.m. on the 26/7/15 and marched from there to AFFRINGUES. JJB	
AFFRINGUES	28/7/15	11.30 a.m.	Left 8 AFFRINGUES for ARQUES by road. JJB	
ARQUES	"	5.30 p.m.	Arrived ARQUES at 5.30 p.m.	
AU SOUVERAIN	29/7/15	3 p.m.	Left ARQUES at 8.30 a.m. arrived AU SOUVERAIN 3 p.m. 29/7/15. DIVISIONAL AMM. COL. HQRS. were established at A LA PROMENADE. JJB	
Do.	31/7/15	9.45 p.m.	Removed DIV. AMM. COL. H.QRS to farm of EMILE DUPONT at AU SOUVERAIN JJB	

REF. MAP to above - HAZEBROUCK 5a.

Henry Beecher Capt A.D.M.
for LT COLONEL R.F.A.
COMMANDING 26th DIVISIONAL AMMUNITION COLUMN.

121/6607

20th Hussars

20th Hus: Ammunition Column.

vol: II

CONFIDENTIAL

Army Form C. 2118.

WAR DIARY
or
INTELLIGENCE SUMMARY.

(Erase heading not required.)

Instructions regarding War Diaries and Intelligence Summaries are contained in F. S. Regs., Part II. and the Staff Manual respectively. Title pages will be prepared in manuscript.

Place	Date	Hour	Summary of Events and Information	Remarks and references to Appendices
Au Souverain	2.8.15		The 16/r and S.A.A. subsections of No 1 Section proceed to Senechal with the 8th D.A.C. 2.T.S.	
"	12.8.15		A Bomb Section is formed under the charge of 2nd Lt. W.H.O. Green R.F.A. 2.T.S.	
"	26.8.15		Nos 2 + 3 Sections will move from billets at Au Souverain to Le Tir Anglais 2.T.S.	
"	28.8.15		do. do. + D.A.C. Hd. Qrs. will move from billets at Au Souverain to billets just out of Estaires on the Neuf Berquin – Estaires Road 2.T.S.	
Estaires	30.8.15		No. 1 Section will return to the Command of the 20th D.A.C. and will move from their billet at Senechal to a billet just out of Estaires on the Neuf Berquin – Estaires Road. 2.T.S.	
Au Souverain	9.8.15		3 G.S. Wagons complete with How. 4.5 ammunition will be transferred from No. 1 Section to A/92 Brigade R.F.A. and the Establishment of the D.A.C. will be permanently reduced accordingly. 2.T.S.	

W. North Lt. Col.
Commdg. 20th Divisional Ammunition Column

121/7595.

30th Hussain

20th Sikh: A.C.
Vol 3
Sept & Oct 15

Confidential

[Stamp: 20th DIVISIONAL AMMUNITION COLUMN, No. ___, Date 3/11/15, R.F.A.]

Officer
C/C, R.A Section.
A.G's Office, 3rd Echelon.

Herewith War Diaries for September & October 1915.

Kindly acknowledge receipt.

2/11/15.

J. R. Foster
LT. COLONEL R.F.A.
COMMANDING 20th DIVISIONAL AMMUNITION COLUMN.

WAR DIARY
INTELLIGENCE SUMMARY. 20th DIV. AMM. COL.

Place	Date	Hour	Summary of Events and Information	Remarks and references to Appendices
Ref. Sheet 36a	1915		R.B.	
L22.C.7.7	Sept 4.		2nd Lt. NUNNELEY R.F.A. & 2nd Lt. A.W. BERTIE R.F.A. were instructed to report for temporary duty to O.C. CROIX BLANCHE GROUP R.F.A.	20/13
	5.		No. 3 Section left the Column for temporary attachment to 8th D.A.C.	20/13
	10.		Two A.V.C. Sergeants arrived for attachment and duty with the Column.	20/13
	12.		Capt. W.C. ROBINSON R.F.A. Commanding No. 2 Section still suffering from an accident to his knee is invalided.	
			Lt. R.G. STAVELEY-DALE R.F.A. from 93rd B.A.C. assumes command of No. 2 Section.	
			2nd Lt. MAHONY R.F.A. from No. 2 Section is posted for duty with the 93rd B.A.C.	20/13
	21.		Owing to forthcoming operations an Ammunition Dump called the PARK DUMP is established at No. 1 Section under the command of Capt. L.A.W. BROOKS R.F.A.	20/13
	26.		No. 3 Section returned to this Column from temporary attachment to the 8th D.A.C. and went into billets at L.9.c.1.2. (Sheet 36A).	
			Capt. W.C. ROBINSON R.F.A. having been invalided home is struck off the strength.	20/13

4 Army Form C. 2118.

WAR DIARY
or
INTELLIGENCE SUMMARY.

20th Div. Amm. Col.

(Erase heading not required.)

Instructions regarding War Diaries and Intelligence Summaries are contained in F. S. Regs., Part II. and the Staff Manual respectively. Title pages will be prepared in manuscript.

Place	Date	Hour	Summary of Events and Information	Remarks and references to Appendices
L.22.c.7.7	1915 Sept 27		The S.A.A. Section of No.2 Section of the 23rd D.A.C. arrived at midnight for temporary attachment to No.2 Section of this Column.	J.W.B.
	30		2nd Lt. R.B. NUNNELEY R.F.A. and 2nd Lt. A.W. BERTIE R.F.A. returned to this Column for duty from the CROIX BLANCHE GROUP R.F.A. Throughout the whole of this month materials were collected and work held in hand in the erection of suitable stables or shelters for the animals of this Column.	J.W.B.

J.W. Booth
LT. COLONEL
COMMANDING 20th DIVISIONAL AMMUNITION COL.

Army Form C. 2118.

WAR DIARY

INTELLIGENCE SUMMARY. 20th DIV AMM. COL.

(Erase heading not required.)

Place	Date	Hour	Summary of Events and Information	Remarks and references to Appendices
L.22.c.7.7	1915 Oct. 1		2nd Lt. A.W. BERTIE R.F.A. is ordered to report at once to R.A. Hd. Qrs. for special duty.	MS
	2		Lt. Col. F. MURRAY-BAILLIE late R.T.O at DIEPPE arrives for Graham attachment.	MS
	5		2nd Lt. A.W. BERTIE R.F.A. is transferred to 92nd Brigade R.F.A.	MS
	6		The S.A.A. Sub-Section of No. 2 Section 23rd D.A.C. attached to this Column for duty returned to 23rd D.A.C. for duty.	MS
	7		No. 89660. R.S.M. BOOCOCK J.H. is suspended from duty on account of incapacity.	MS
			No. 35940. B.S.M. BECKHAM J.J. from a/B.&M.S. C/90 Bde R.F.A. assumed the duties of R.S.M. of this Column	MS
	11		2nd Lt. J.H. BOOTHBY R.F.A. is posted to No.1 Section of the Column from the 92nd Brigade R.F.A.	MS
	13		Lt. Col. F. MURRAY-BAILLIE left for England on leave.	MS
			2nd Lt. R.G.L. ROBERTSON R.F.A. is posted to No. 2 Section of the Column from C/92nd Brigade R.F.A.	MS

WAR DIARY
INTELLIGENCE SUMMARY.   20th DIV. AMM. COL.

Army Form C. 2118.

Place	Date	Hour	Summary of Events and Information	Remarks and references to Appendices
L.22.c.7.7	1915			
	02.13		2nd Lt. R.B. NUNNELEY R.F.A. is transferred from No.3 Section to C/92nd Brigade R.F.A.	MJS
	17		Orders were given for the PARK DUMP to be gradually exhausted and done away with.	MJS
	22		Capt. L.A.W. BROOKS R.F.A. proceeds to England on leave. No. 89.660 R.S.M. BOOCOCK J.H. is ordered to proceed to HAVRE and to report to O.C. Reinforcements on arrival and is accordingly struck off the strength of this Column.	
			2nd Lt. C.H.M. PEARSON R.F.A. assumes command of No.1 Section during the absence on leave of Capt. L.A.W. BROOKS R.F.A.	MJS
	25		50 N.C.Os and men from this Column are detailed to Batteries for instruction in Gunnery and are replaced by the same number from the R.F.A. Brigades.	MJS
	26		2nd Lt. J.H. BOOTHBY R.F.A. is struck off the strength with effect from the 17th inst. on his appointment to the 21st LANCERS.	MJS

WAR DIARY
INTELLIGENCE SUMMARY. 20th DIV. AMM. COL.

Army Form C. 2118.

Place	Date	Hour	Summary of Events and Information	Remarks and references to Appendices
L.22.c.7.7.	1915 Oct. 27		All returns and indents for BOMBS, GRENADES etc. will in future be submitted direct by the O.C. BOMB SECTION to the D.A. Q.M.G. of this Division who will be responsible for their supplies.	
	28		LT. R. C. RUSSELL R.F.A. having reported from England for duty is posted to No. 3 Section	
	31		Throughout the whole of this month great progress was made in the erection of stables and shelters etc. for the animals of this Column. During the month the stables were visited and inspected by the D.A. & Q.M.G. 3rd CORPS who was satisfied with the progress made.	

M.D. Foster
LT. COLONEL R.F.A.
COMMANDING 20th DIVISIONAL AMMUNITION COLUMN

Johannessen

2 h Sitte.
fol: 4

131/7678

a/age

Nov 15.

WAR DIARY

20th Div. Amm. Col. R.F.A.

INTELLIGENCE SUMMARY.

(Erase heading not required.)

November 1915.

Place	Date	Hour	Summary of Events and Information	Remarks and references to Appendices
Sheet 36A	1915 Nov. 1		Capt. L.A.W. Brooks R.F.A. returned from one weeks leave and resumed Command of No. 1 Section.	J.J.B.
	10		A Court of Inquiry was held at No. 1 Section to inquire into the circumstances of a self inflicted injury to a man attached to No. 1 Section. The man in question was sent back to his own unit for trial by Court Martial.	J.J.B.
C.7.7.	11		2nd Lt. R.E. Rawson R.F.A. having arrived is posted to No. 1 Section.	J.J.B.
	17		Capt. R.S. Henderson R.F.A. returned from one week leave and resumed Command of No. 3 Section.	J.J.B.
C.2.2.	18		Lt. Col. J.R. Foster R.F.A., Capt. & Adjt. F.P. Belcher R.F.A., 2nd Lt. J.M. Petersen R.F.A., 2nd Lt. H.H. Munro R.F.A. together with 4 N.C.Os. & 36 men of the Column underwent a Gas Test at the Bomb Section satisfactorily.	J.J.B.
	20		2nd Lt. W.H.O. Green R.F.A. is appointed Divisional Trench Mortar Officer in addition to his duties as Divisional Bomb Officer.	J.J.B.
I.7.	23		The G.O.C. R.A. 20th Division inspected the Column in full marching order — and he considered the turn out very satisfactory.	J.J.B.
	24		2nd Lt. M.W. Richards R.F.A. having arrived is posted to No. 1 Section - Supernumerary.	J.J.B.

WAR DIARY 20th DIV. AMM COL. R.F.A.

INTELLIGENCE SUMMARY. NOVEMBER 1915 Contd.

Army Form C. 2118.

(Erase heading not required.)

Place	Date	Hour	Summary of Events and Information	Remarks and references to Appendices
	1915 Nov.27		Lt. A.S. WALL R.A.M.C. having reported for duty assumes medical charge of the Column vice Lt. E.S. JOHNSON R.A.M.C. transferred. F/S.	
	28		Lt. Col. J.R. FOSTER R.F.A. having proceeded on 7 days leave Capt. R.S. HENDERSON R.F.A. assumes command of the Column F/S.	
	29		Capt. J.B. PARRY R.F.A. having arrived will take over the command of the Column from Capt. R.S. HENDERSON R.F.A. until the return of Lt. Col. T.R. FOSTER R.F.A. from leave. F/S.	
	30		The D.D.R. inspected all the horse & mules of the Column and expressed great satisfaction as to their condition. F/S. During the month each Officer attended one lecture on Court Martial Procedure at ERQUINGHEM by Capt. CLARK. F/S. The party of 50 N.C.O.s taken from this Column for attachment to Brigades for instruction in gunnery for a fortnight at a time was continued throughout this month. The same number of N.C.O.s taken from Brigade temporarily being attached to the Column for the same periods. F/S.	

J.N. Foster
LT. COLONEL R.F.A.
COMMANDING 20th DIVISIONAL AMMUNITION COLUMN

26/2 8.M.
btl. 5-

121/7931

Confidential

WAR DIARY
20th DIV. AMM. COL. R.F.A.
INTELLIGENCE SUMMARY. DECEMBER. 1915

Army Form C. 2118.

Place	Date	Hour	Summary of Events and Information	Remarks and references to Appendices
	1915			
	Dec 3		Capt. L.A.W. BROOKS, R.F.A. Commanding No 1 Section was reported sick and sent to hospital. 2nd Lt. C.H.M PEARSON R.F.A in temporary command of the Section.	D.113
	6		2nd Lt A.T. GULLIVER R.F.A. arrived from the 93rd Bde. R.F.A and assumed the temporary command of No 1 Section.	D.115
	7		2nd Lt. R.E. RAWSON R.F.A of No 1 Section to be attached to 93rd Bde during the same period. Lt. Col. J.R. FOSTER R.A. having returned from leave resumes command of the Column.	D.115 D.113
	10		There was a Route March for the Column in full marching order for about 4 miles — the equipment and turnout being satisfactory.	D.113
	13		Lt. T.A. CODNER, R.F.A. having arrived from the 93rd Bde R.F.A. is posted to the Command of No. 1 Section.	D.113.
	14		Capt. F.P. BELCHER, R.F.A. Adjutant departed for England on 7 days leave. Capt. R.G. STAVELEY-DALE, R.F.A. performing the duties of Adjutant during his absence on leave of Capt. BELCHER. Capt. J.B. PARRY, R.F.A. to command No. 2 Section during the period that Capt. R.G. STAVELEY-DALE is acting Adjutant. The horses & mules of the Column were inspected by the A.D.V.S. of the Division.	D.113. D.139 D.139

Army Form C. 2118.

WAR DIARY
or
INTELLIGENCE SUMMARY.

20th Div Amm Col RFA
DECEMBER 1915

(Erase heading not required.)

Place	Date	Hour	Summary of Events and Information	Remarks and references to Appendices
	1915			
	Dec. 15		Capt. L.A.W. BROOKS, R.F.A. having been invalided to England is struck off the strength. JJJJ	
	22		No. 70280 Driver M. McLEAN of No. 2 Section was tried by F.G.C.M. at D.A.C. Hd. Qrs. President - Major J.A. BUTCHART, R.F.A. Members - Capt. T.B. PARRY, R.F.A. 2nd Lt. C.H.M. PEARSON, R.F.A. - on the charge of being 1. Absent from picket without permission of his superior officer and 2. Drunkenness - he was found guilty and sentenced to 3 months field punishment No. 1. JJJJ	
	23		Capt. F.P. BELCHER, R.F.A. returned from leave and resumed his duties as Adjutant. JJJJ 2nd Lt. A.T. GULLIVER, R.F.A. and 2nd Lt. C.H.M. PEARSON, R.F.A. proceeded to England on 7 days leave. JJJJ	
	24		No. 70183 Driver E. HOUGHTON of No. 2 Section was accidentally run over by a motor cycle and motor lorry and was taken to hospital where he died next day. The motor cyclist gave the name of J.A.H. MILLER of the R.E. XXth Division but no such man could be found. JJJJ	

Confidential

WAR DIARY
20th DIV. AMM. COL. R.F.A.
or
INTELLIGENCE SUMMARY

Army Form C. 2118.

DECEMBER 1915.

(Erase heading not required.)

Instructions regarding War Diaries and Intelligence Summaries are contained in F. S. Regs., Part II. and the Staff Manual respectively. Title pages will be prepared in manuscript.

Place	Date	Hour	Summary of Events and Information	Remarks and references to Appendices
	1915 Dec 27		A Court of Inquiry was held at D.A.C. Hd. Qrs. to inquire into the circumstances under which No. 70183 Driver E. HOUGHTON met his death — the finding was that it was due to his own negligence, but that the consequences in all probability would not have been so serious had not the motor cyclist (who could not be found) been travelling at an excessive speed. App.1.	
	29		Capt. R.S. HENDERSON, R.F.A. Commanding No.3 Section being considered incompetent for the Command of a Unit in the R.F.A. returned to England under orders from Army Headquarters to report in writing to the War Office on arrival. App.2. Lt. W. LAING, R.F.A. having arrived from 92nd Bde R.F.A. is posted to the Command of No.3 Section. App.3. Lt. R.G. RUSSELL, R.F.A. proceeded to Scotland on 7 days leave. App.3. Lt. R.G. RUSSELL, R.F.A. was transferred from No.3 Section to No. 2 Section. 2nd Lt. R.C.L. ROBERTSON, R.F.A. was transferred from No. 2 Section to No.3 Section. App.3.	
	31		Lectures were given during the month by qualified Officers of the Column to the Subaltern Officers of the Column on — Military Law — Stable Management — and Conduct. App.3.	

L.N. Twate?
LT. COLONEL R.F.A.
COMMANDING 20th DIVISIONAL AMMUNITION COLUMN

Lit. S. A.
vol 6

SECRET

WAR DIARY 20th Div. Amm. Col. R.F.A. Army Form C. 2118.

INTELLIGENCE SUMMARY.

JANUARY — 1916.

(Erase heading not required.)

Place	Date	Hour	Summary of Events and Information	Remarks and references to Appendices
	1916			
	1 Jan.		2nd Lt. M.W. RICHARDS R.F.A. is transferred from No.3 Section to No.1 Section	
			2nd Lt. C.H.M. PEARSON R.F.A. do No.1 do to No.3 do	L. 243.
	7 "		No. 61896 Driver W. ORR of No.1 Section was tried by F.G.C.M. at 91st Bde. Hd. Qrs. for overstaying his leave — found guilty and sentenced to 3 months hard labour — the sentence was commuted by C.R.A. to 28 days F.P. No.1.	243.
Shet to 36	9 "		Capt. J.B. PARRY, R.F.A. having been transferred to England is ordered to report in writing to the WAR OFFICE on arrival.	243.
			2nd Lt. J.M. PETERSON R.F.A. is struck off the strength with effect from 31/12/15 having been invalided to England.	243.
	12 "		Lt. A.T. GULLIVER R.F.A. is transferred from A/93 Brigade to D.A.C. and posted to No.1 Section	243.
	15 "		The D.D.R. 1st ARMY inspected the whole of the horse transport in the Column in a field adjoining Column Hd. Qrs.	243.
	19 "		Lt. Col. J.R. FOSTER R.A. and Capt. R.C. Stansley-Dale attended a Court Martial at D.M.T.	243.
	20 "		2nd Lt. R.E. RAWSON R.F.A. on return from attached 93rd Bde. to Tucker K.T.D. Bowl Section for instruction.	243.

SECRET.

WAR DIARY 20th DIV AMM. COL. R.F.A. Army Form C. 2118.

or

INTELLIGENCE SUMMARY. JANUARY 1916.

(Erase heading not required.)

Place	Date	Hour	Summary of Events and Information	Remarks and references to Appendices
	1916			
ESTAIRES	11 Jan.	9 p.m.	A Bomb Section left their Magazine of Stores in charge of a Guard and proceeded to MORBECQUE being attached to the 60th Infantry Brigade.	873.B.
do.	21 Jan. 12 Midnight		The Guard at Bomb Magazine Store was relieved by the 8th Div. who took over the stock of Bombs etc.	873.
		10 a.m.	The 61st Trench Mortar Battery arrived for attachment to the Column until further orders.	873.
	22 Jan.	8 a.m.	The Column marched out to join the rest of the Division to join the II Army - arrived LETIR + NCLAIS, HAZEBROUCK at 1 p.m. and bivouaced for the night.	873
		4 p.m.	The 60th Trench Mortar Battery arrived at about 4 p.m. for attachment to the Column until further orders.	873.
		3 p.m.	The Bomb Section reported their arrival from MORBECQUE.	873.
HAZEBROUCK	23 Jan.	8 a.m.	The Column consisting of H. Qrs. Nos 1, 2, 3 Sections Bomb Section and 60th + 61st Trench Mortar Batteries continued their march arriving at LEDERZEELE at about 4 p.m.	873.

SECRET.

WAR DIARY 20th DIV AMM COL. RFA
INTELLIGENCE SUMMARY. January 1916.

Army Form C. 2118.

Place	Date 1916	Hour	Summary of Events and Information	Remarks and references to Appendices
LEDERZEELE	Jan 24	10.30 am	The G.O.C. & C.R.A. 20th Division visited the Column.	J.J.B.
	27		The Division being in rest, 2 guns were placed at the disposal of the Column by the 91st Brigade R.F.A. each day 11.30 - 12.30 am & 3.30 - 4.30 pm for instruction of Officers and N.C.Os.	J.J.B.
	28		Parties from each section & Bomb section were sent to R.F.A. Headquarters at NOORD PEENE & to be arranged from time in [???] to take over duties of Camp Guard at the 49th Division M.T.	J.J.B.
	29		2nd Lt. W.H.O. Green R.F.A. proceeded on leave to England for 10 days. 2nd Lt. R.E. Rawson R.F.A. to command the Bomb section during the absence of 2nd Lt. W.H.O. GREEN, R.F.A.	J.J.B.
	31		The D.D.R 2nd ARMY inspected the whole of the animals in the Column and found them to his entire satisfaction.	J.J.B.

L.A.Troter
Lt. Col.
Comndg. 20th DIV. AMM. COL. RFA.

20ᵗʰ ᵴ A.C.
vol 7

Confidential

WAR DIARY
INTELLIGENCE SUMMARY
(Erase heading not required.)

FEBRUARY 1916.

Army Form C. 2118.

20th DIV. AMM COL. R.F.A.

Instructions regarding War Diaries and Intelligence Summaries are contained in F. S. Regs., Part II. and the Staff Manual respectively. Title pages will be prepared in manuscript.

Place	Date 1916	Hour	Summary of Events and Information	Remarks and references to Appendices
LEDERZEELE	Feb. 1.		The French Interpreter Lance Corpl. E. ROUAUD attached is posted to the 49th Division.	F798
"	3		Advance parties moved from the LEDERZEELE area to the ARNEKE area.	F798
ARNEKE	4		The Column moved from LEDERZEELE ARNEKE – the Bomb Section being established at ESQUELBECQ.	F798
"	7		2nd Lt. W.H.O. GREEN, R.F.A. having returned from leave resumes command of the Bomb Section. F798. M. Interpreter LE BLON (Belgian) is taken on the strength of the Column as transferred from the 49th Division.	F798
"	10		Lt. LAING, R.F.A. Commanding No. 3 Section proceeded to England on 7 days leave. 2nd Lt. C.H.M. PEARSON, R.F.A. assumes command of No. 3 Section during the absence on leave of Lt. LAING, R.F.A.	F798
"	11		The Adjutant (Capt. F.P. BELCHER, R.F.A.) rode over to POPERINGHE to interview the C.O. 14th D.A.C. 2nd Lt. R.E. RAWSON, R.F.A. proceeded to England on 7 days leave.	F798 F798
"	13		Advance parties were sent from each Section under the command of Lt. GULLIVER R.F.A. to the POPERINGHE area to take over the camps lately occupied by the 14th D.A.C.	F798

Confidential

WAR DIARY

INTELLIGENCE SUMMARY.
(Erase heading not required.)

FEBRUARY 1916

Army Form C. 2118.

17

20th DIV. AMM. COL. R.F.A.

Place	Date	Hour	Summary of Events and Information	Remarks and references to Appendices
	1916			
ARNEKE	Feb. 14		The Column moved from the ARNEKE area to the POPERINGHE area in the early hours of the morning. J.73.B	
A.18.c.6.2. (Sheet 28)	14		No.1 Section take up their position at A.18.c.6.2. (Sheet 28) as an Advanced Section supplying the whole of the ammunition requirements of the Division – horses from Brigade Ammunition Column fetching the ammunition. J.73.B	
			The Bomb Section also take up their position at this place. J.73.B The rear Sections being employed on fatigue work for the Division. J.73.B	
HAMHOEK	14		2nd Lt. M.W. RICHARDS, R.F.A. proceeded to England on 7 days leave. J.73.B Lt. LAING, R.F.A. having returned from leave resumes Command of No. 3 Section. J.73.B	
	19		2nd Lt. R.E. RAWSON, R.F.A. returned from leave. J.73.B Lt. H.H. MUNRO, R.F.A. and 2nd Lt. C.H.M. PEARSON, R.F.A. proceeded on a fortnights Field Artillery Course at BERTHEN. J.73.B	
	20		2nd Lt. E.A. SMITH R.F.A. (S.R.) having arrived from England is posted to No. 2 Section. J.73.B	

CONFIDENTIAL

WAR DIARY
INTELLIGENCE SUMMARY of 20 DIV. AMM. COL. R.F.A.

FEBRUARY 1916

Army Form C. 2118.

18

Place	Date 1916	Hour	Summary of Events and Information	Remarks and references to Appendices
HANHOEK	Feb. 26		Lt. LAING, R.F.A. is ordered to report to 90th Brigade Headquarters for temporary special duty owing to casualties. J.J.S. 2nd Lt. ROBERTSON R.F.A. will Command No. 3 Section during the absence of Lt. LAING, R.F.A. J.J.S.	
	28		2nd Lt. M.W. RICHARDS, R.F.A. returned from leave. J.J.S.	
	29		2nd Lt. ROBERTSON, R.F.A. proceeded to BERTHEN on a Trench Mortar Course. J.J.S. 2nd Lt. SMITH, R.F.A. from No. 2 Section to temporarily command No. 3 Section. J.J.S.	

2/3/16.

[signature]
LT. COLONEL R.F.A.
COMMANDING 20th DIVISIONAL AMMUNITION COLUMN.

Confidential

WAR DIARY 20th DIV AMM. COL. RFA   Army Form C. 2118.

or

INTELLIGENCE SUMMARY. MARCH — 1916

(Erase heading not required.)

Place	Date 1916	Hour	Summary of Events and Information	Remarks and references to Appendices
HANNHOEK	Mch. 3		Temp. Lt. W. LAING. R.F.A promoted temporary Captain with effect from 27/1/16.	
	4		Temp. Lt. H.H. Munro R.F.A returned from a Field Artillery Course at BERTHEN. J.P.B.	
			Temp. Capt. LAING, R.F.A having returned from the temporary command of a Battery in the 92nd (Howitzer) Brigade resumes Command of No. 3 Section. J.P.B.	
			2nd Lt. E.H. SMITH, R.F.A returns to No. 2 Section from No. 3 Section.	
			2nd Lt. C.H.M. PEARSON and 2nd Lt. C.G.L. ROBERTSON reported their return from Special Courses. J.P.B.	
	5		Lt. R.G. RUSSELL R.F.A. to be attached for duty to No. 1 Section	
	13		2nd Lt. M.W. RICHARDS, R.F.A. to be attached for duty to No. 2 Section. J.P.B.	
			Lt. H.H. MUNRO R.F.A. to temporarily command No. 2 Section. J.P.B.	
	16		The following Casualties occurred between 6th & 12th whilst attached to D/93 Battery: — 1 Killed — 1 died of wounds, 2 wounded. J.P.B.	
	17		Lt. F.C. ROSS-BROWN R.F.A is appointed to temporarily command No 2 Section J.P.B.	
			By orders of the Second Army the wagons of the Column were reduced to 28 per Section — the surplus wagons being lent to the 1st & 2nd Canadian Divisions. J.P.B.	

Confidential

WAR DIARY 20th DIV AMM COL R.F.A. Army Form C. 2118.
INTELLIGENCE SUMMARY. MARCH - 1916
(Erase heading not required.) 20

Place	Date	Hour	Summary of Events and Information	Remarks and references to Appendices
HUNHOEK	1916 Mch 18		Lt. R.G. RUSSELL. R.F.A. Transferred from No.1 Section to 93rd Brigade R.F.A. 2nd Lt. C.H.M. PEARSON. R.F.A. do " 90th Brigade R.F.A. 2nd Lt. M.W. RICHARDS. R.F.A. do " attached to No.1 Section	9735
	20		" " " " attached No.2 Section Capt. W. LAING. R.F.A. proceeded to ENGLAND on a Field Artillery Course	9735
	24		2nd Lt. C.G.L. ROBERTSON. R.F.A. assuming command of No.3 Section in his absence. Lt. Col. T.R. FOSTER. R.A. proceeded on leave for 10 days - Capt. F.P. BELCHER. R.F.A. assuming command of the Column in his absence.	9735
	25		2nd Lt. R.E. RAWSON. R.F.A. from attached No.1 Section re-attached to No.3 Section 2nd Lt. E.H. SMITH. R.F.A. will return to No.2 Section from attached No.3 Section	9735
	27		Information has been received from the BASE that Capt. R.G. STAVELEY-DALE's leave has been extended to 8/4/16 by Medical Board assembled by order of War Office	9735
	26		No.70094 Bomb. E. PLUNKETT of No.1 Section did of wounds received in action some say whilst attached to Right Group Artillery.	9735
	21		Lt. F.C. ROSS-BROWN. R.F.A. left for attachment to 93rd Brigade R.F.A. to command a Battery for a week — Lt. H.H. MUNRO. R.F.A. Commanding No.2 Section in his absence.	9735

Confidential

WAR DIARY
or
INTELLIGENCE SUMMARY.

20th Div Amm Col. R.F.A. Army Form C. 2118.

MARCH – 1916

21

Place	Date	Hour	Summary of Events and Information	Remarks and references to Appendices
	1916			
HANNOER	Mch. 28		Lt. F.C. ROSS-BROWN R.F.A. having returned from attached 93rd Brigade R.F.A. resumed command of No. 2 Section. DAC.	
	31		Capt. T.A. CODNER R.F.A. having departed for England for 7 days leave Lt. A.T. GULLIVER R.F.A. assumed command of No. 1 Section. DAC. Capt. B.E. WALL R.A.M.C. having departed for England for 7 days leave Capt. H.S. MULLON R.A.M.C. took over medical charge of the Column. DAC. During the whole of this month No. 1 Section being in the advanced position attended to all the ammunition requirements of the Division by means of a large Dump – the Brigade Ammunition Columns filling up from the Dump. The rear Sections (Nos 1 & 2) performed R.E. fatigue duties for the Division. DAC The process of gradually replacing all the horses L.D. and H.D. in the Sections by mules was continued. DAC. Poor progress was made in the Signalling, telephone & linesmen classes. DAC. During the month there was a marked decrease in the sick in the Column – men and animals. DAC.	11/4/16. A.N. Foster Lt. Col. Commanding 20th D.A.C.

CONFIDENTIAL

Army Form C. 2118. Vol 9
22

WAR DIARY 20th DIV AMM COL. RFA

INTELLIGENCE SUMMARY. APRIL — 1916.

(Erase heading not required.)

Place	Date	Hour	Summary of Events and Information	Remarks and references to Appendices
HANNOEN, BOEZINGHE	1916 Ap. 4		Capt. W. LAING, R.F.A. having returned from a Course at Larkhill resumes command of No. 3 Section. 7.7.8. Lt. Col. J. R. FOSTER R.A. having returned from leave resumed command of the Column. 7.7.8.	
	7.		Lt. F.C. ROSS-BROWN, R.F.A. and 2nd Lt. C.G.L. ROBERTSON, R.F.A. proceeded to England on 7 days leave. 2.7.8. Lt. H.H. MUNRO, R.F.A. to command No. 2 Section during the absence on leave of Lt. ROSS-BROWN R.F.A. 7.7.8. Lt. F.C. ROSS-BROWN, R.F.A. having returned from leave resumes command of No. 2 Section. 2.7.8.	
	16.		2nd Lt. C.G.L. ROBERTSON R.F.A. returned from leave. 7.7.8. It having been decided to hold a divisional Horse Show when the Division moves into Reserve Capt. T.A. COONER R.F.A. is selected to represent the Column on the Committee. 7.7.8.	
	17		Lt. H.H. MURNO, R.F.A. proceeded to ZEGGERS CAPPEL on behalf of the Column to take over a stock of gun & Howitzer ammunition from the 6th Division. 7.7.8.	

Sheet 27

CONFIDENTIAL

WAR DIARY
20th DIV. AMM. COL. R.F.A.
Army Form C. 2118.

INTELLIGENCE SUMMARY.
APRIL — 1916

(Erase heading not required.)

23

Place	Date	Hour	Summary of Events and Information	Remarks and references to Appendices
HONDSCHOOTE	1916 April 18		The Adjutant Capt. P.P. BELCHER, R.F.A. proceeded to the Reserve Area around RUBROUCK to make arrangements for billetting the Column. ⅔⅞.	
	19	At 2 pm	the Column consisting of Headquarters, No. 2 Section and No. 3 Section moved off to the Reserve Area and arrived at BOLLEZEELE at 10.45 pm. No. 1 Section having confirmed their order, only joined the Column at this place owing to the units of the 6th Division not having moved out of the billets at RUBROUCK the Column was compelled to bivouac for the night at BOLLEZEELE — moving off subsequently to their billets around RUBROUCK at 10 am on the 20th April 1916. ⅔⅞.	
BOLLEZEELE				
RUBROUCK	20		Column Headquarters was established in RUBROUCK. ⅔⅞. The Band Section moved to the Reserve Area on the 18th & 19th April on direct orders from Divisional Headquarters. ⅔⅞.	
	18 & 19th		Officers & men of the 6th D.A.C. arrived at the Sections to take over ammunition and camp stores prior to our moving to the Reserve Area. ⅔⅞.	

CONFIDENTIAL

WAR DIARY 20th DIV. AMM. COL. R.F.A.

INTELLIGENCE SUMMARY. APRIL — 1916.

(Erase heading not required.)

Army Form C. 2118.

Place	Date	Hour	Summary of Events and Information	Remarks and references to Appendices
RUBROUCK	1916 Apl 25		A Special telephone class assembled at this Headquarters under R.E. hospitallers consisting of 30 men from this Column. 20 men from the 4 R.A. Brigades and 3 men from the Field Ambulance.	379.9
	27		Lt. A.T. GULLIVER R.F.A. and Lt. H.H. MUNRO R.F.A. proceeded on leave to Scotland and England respectively.	379.9
	28		2nd Lt. W.H.O. GREEN. R.F.A. proceeded on leave to England. R.F.A. 2nd Lt. R.E. RAWSON R.F.A. commanding the Bomb section during the absence on leave of 2nd Lt. W.H.O. GREEN R.F.A.	373.9
	29		2nd Lt. C.G.L. ROBERTSON R.F.A. proceeded to the Bomb Section for 1 months training to fit him to take over command of the Section.	373.9
	30		During the month the Column was inspected on foot parade in full marching order by the O.C. Lectures on various subjects for Officers were given at Headquarters whilst in the line. 50/60 N.C.O's and men were sent to the Brigades for the purpose of preparing advanced gun positions.	373.9 373.9

Carter

● CONFIDENTIAL

WAR DIARY 20th DIV. AMM. COL. R.F.A. Army Form C. 2118.

INTELLIGENCE SUMMARY. APRIL - 1916.

25

(Erase heading not required.)

Instructions regarding War Diaries and Intelligence Summaries are contained in F. S. Regs., Part II. and the Staff Manual respectively. Title pages will be prepared in manuscript.

Place	Date	Hour	Summary of Events and Information	Remarks and references to Appendices
	1916 Apl 30		Whilst in the line 24 wagons were sent to Infantry Brigades many of them being returned in a bad state of repair - very little care being taken of them. 2733. Jun 16/20 wagons were also turned out daily for R.E. fatigues - 2748. Some progress was made in the training of small squads of signallers. 2713. The L.D. and H.D. horses were previously taken from the column by order of the D.D.R. 2nd Army and replaced by mules. 2733. Throughout the month a marked improvement was shown in the health of the men. 2749. W Brohn Lt.Col. Comdg. 20th D.A.C.	

1577 Wt.W10791/1773 500,000 1/15 D. D. & L. A.D.S.S./Forms/C. 2118.

Confidential

WAR DIARY
of
INTELLIGENCE SUMMARY.
(Erase heading not required.)

20th Div. Ammn Col. RFA
MAY 1916 Vol 16

Place	Date	Hour	Summary of Events and Information	Remarks and references to Appendices
RUBROUCK Sheet 27.	1916 May 5		Tempy. Capt. R.G. STAVELEY-DALE, RFA is struck off the strength with effect from 2 March 1916. JJS	
			No. 83916 Driver GEORGE COVENEY of No. 3 Section was awarded the D.C.M. JJS	
		6	No. 70193 Gunner JOHN HAGUE of No. 2 Section " " Military Medal. JJS	
			Capt. F.P. BELCHER, RFA proceeded to England on leave JJS.	
			Lt. F.C. ROSS-BROWN, RFA assumed the duties of Adjutant during the absence on leave of Capt. BELCHER. JJS	
		12–15.	Arrangements were made to re-organise the Column viz, the abolition of Brigade Ammunition Columns in the D.A.C. all surplus Officers, N.C.O's men, also animals, harness and carts to go to the Base, Calais when the reorganisation is completed JJS. The Column was reformed into 4 sections, with the following Officers as Section Commanders:—	
			No. 1 Section – Capt. WRIGHT, RFA	
			No. 2 " – Capt. CODNER, RFA	
			No. 3 " – Capt. WALKER, RFA	
			No. 4 Section – Capt. LAING, RFA JJS	

Confidential
WAR DIARY 20th Div. Amm. Col RFA Army Form C. 2118.
or
INTELLIGENCE SUMMARY. May 1916

27

Place	Date	Hour	Summary of Events and Information	Remarks and references to Appendices
RUBROUCK	1916 May 16		Lt. R.G. RUSSELL RFA has been appointed Commander Base Details. JWB Capt. F.P. BELCHER. RFA returned from leave and resumed the duties of Adjutant. JWB	
	19		The Base Details party under the command of 2nd Lt. RICHARDSON (Richards) left by road for the Base, Calais. JWB. Lt. R.G. RUSSELL RFA proceeded to Base, Calais by train. JWB After having sent Advance Parties early on the morning of the 19th inst. to PESELHOEK, POPERINGHE, to take over from the GUARDS D.A.C. the Column left the RUBROUCK area at 5 am under the command of Lt. Col. J.R. FOSTER. R.A. and proceeded to PESELHOEK arriving there at about 1.30 p.m. being responsible for the ammunition supply for the division from 6 p.m. 20th May 1916. JWB	
	20		It was arranged to work the ammunition supply from a Central dump at D.A.C. Hd. Qrs. under being made to section and sections delivering to Battery gun positions and infantry Brigade Transport lines. JWB	

Confidential

WAR DIARY 20th Div. Amm. Col. RFA
or
INTELLIGENCE SUMMARY

Army Form C. 2118.

(Erase heading not required.)

May 1916.

Place	Date	Hour	Summary of Events and Information	Remarks and references to Appendices
	1916			
PESELHOEK.	May 21		2nd Lt. P. de L. DYSON-SKINNER R.F.A. is struck off the strength.	J.T.B.
POPERINGHE.			2nd Lts. E. H. R. FARRELL and J. B. GREENE having arrived are posted to Nos. 4 and 3 Sections respectively with effect from the 20th inst.	J.T.B.
Sheet 28.	23		The Corps Comm. under Lt. Gen. LORD CAVAN - visited the Column accompanied by the 14th Corps D.A.A. and Q.M.G. (Brig. Gen. COOKE)	J.T.B.
	28		Lt. H. H. MUNRO. R.F.A. proceeded to England on Special Leave	J.T.B.
	29		Capt. W. LAING, R.F.A. and Lt. B. G. TWYCROSS R.F.A. proceeded to England on 10 days leave.	J.T.B.
			The D.A.A. & Q.M.G. O'Brien (Lt. Col. DUNDAS) visited the Column	#J.T.B.
			Capt. BELCHER, R.F.A. was appointed Town Major of POPERINGHE during the absence on leave of Capt. COLLINS	J.T.B.
			Lt. A. T. GULLIVER, R.F.A. was appointed to perform the duties of Adjutant during the absence on special duty of Capt. BELCHER.	J.T.B.
	30		The Lt. Col. Commanding inspected the respective Camps of the Sections and Headquarters and found everything in order.	J.T.B.
			Capt. Wright R.F.A. Commanding No. 1 Section having been appointed carried	J.T.B.

Confidential

WAR DIARY 20th Div. Amm. Col. R.F.A.
or
INTELLIGENCE SUMMARY.

Army Form C. 2118.

May 1916.

29

Place	Date	Hour	Summary of Events and Information	Remarks and references to Appendices
PESCHOEK	1916 May 30		Contd. — Constant Instruction in Equitation to Second Army afforded on the 31st May to take up his new duties — Lt. W.J. Hill R.F.A. of No. 2 Section being appointed to temporarily command No. 1 Section. J/38 2nd Lt. J.B. Green R.F.A. was attached for duty to No. 2 Section from No. 3 Section. J/38	
POPERINGHE Shl 28.	31.		Lt. H.H. Munro R.F.A. proceeded to England on 10 days special leave of absence on 28th May 1916. J/38 2nd Lt. R.K. Brydon R.F.A. having arrived is taken on the strength and posted to No. 2 Section. J/38	

LAllroy Lt. Col. R.A.
Commdg. 20th D.A.C.

Confidential

Vol 11

WAR DIARY

20th Div. Ammn. Col. RFA

Army Form C. 2118.

INTELLIGENCE SUMMARY.

JUNE 1916.

(Erase heading not required.)

30.

Instructions regarding War Diaries and Intelligence Summaries are contained in F. S. Regs., Part II. and the Staff Manual respectively. Title pages will be prepared in manuscript.

Place	Date	Hour	Summary of Events and Information	Remarks and references to Appendices
	1916			
PESELHOEK	May 31		No. 3 Section moves to new position at VLAMATINGHE. JJB	
	June 1		No. 1 Section do. do. JJB	
		2	2nd Lt. W.E. KICK, RFA proceeded to England on 7 days leave.	
			2nd Lt. J.B. GREENE, RFA was posted from No.3 Section to 92nd Bde. RFA. JJB	
		3	Capt. A.E. WRIGHT, RFA appointed Assistant Instructor of Gunnery 2nd Army. JJB	
			Capt. F.C. ROSS-BROWN, RFA to command No.1 Section vice Capt. WRIGHT	
			Lt. W.J. HILL, RFA to command No. 4 Section during absence on leave of Capt. LAING.	
			2nd Lt. H.G.W. GODFREY, RFA posted from No.4 Section to 92nd Bde. RFA	
			No. 4 Section lost a G.S. Wagon destroyed by shell fire near YPRES – 2 mules slightly injured. JJB	
		4	2nd Lt. R.E. RAWSON, RFA granted 10 days special leave of absence. JJB	
		5	No. 1 Section had 5 horses killed by shell fire in their lines. JJB	
		6	No. 3 Section had a driver slightly wounded. JJB	
		7	1 Gunner killed by shell fire.	
			Capt. T.A. CODNER, RFA and 2nd Lt. WYER, RFA granted 7 days leave.	
			Capt. W. LAING, RFA & Lt. TWYCROSS, RFA rejoined from leave. JJB	

Confidential   WAR DIARY 20th DIV. AMM. COL. RFA   Army Form C. 2118.

INTELLIGENCE SUMMARY.   JUNE. 1916.

31

Place	Date	Hour	Summary of Events and Information	Remarks and references to Appendices
PESELHOEK	1916 June 7		Capt. W. LAING. RFA. assumed command of No. 4 Section. 2798	
			Lt. W.J. HILL RFA to command No. 2 Section during absence on leave of Capt. CODNER 2798	
			No. 3 Section had an A.S.C. horse wounded and shot next day. 2798	
	8		No. 3 Section had one horse killed in YPRES 2798	
			No. 1 & 3 Sections removed their horse lines from VLAMERTINGHE owing to heavy shelling to G.4.d.4.4. and G.3.d. (Sheet 28) respectively, leaving their ammunition dumps at H.1.d.3.0 and H.8.a.4.9. (Sheet 28) respectively. 2798	
	10		Capt. F.P. BELCHER. RFA assumed the duties of Adjutant on the return of the Town Major of POPERINGHE from leave. 2798	
			Lt. Col. T.R. FOSTER. RFA proceeded on 7 days leave of absence. 2798	
	12		Capt. E.M. WALKER. RFA to command the Column during the absence on leave of Lt. Col. FOSTER. RFA. 2798	
	13		No. 2 Section lost a G.S. Wagon near YPRES. 2798	
			2nd Lieuts. J.C. HUNTER, RFA and V.V. FABER, RFA proceeded on 7 days leave. 2798	
	15		Capt. CODNER RFA resumed command of No. 2 Section on return from leave. 2798	

Confidential

WAR DIARY 20th DIV. AMM. COL. R.F.A.

Army Form C. 2118.

INTELLIGENCE SUMMARY. JUNE. 1916.

32

Instructions regarding War Diaries and Intelligence Summaries are contained in F. S. Regs., Part II. and the Staff Manual respectively. Title pages will be prepared in manuscript.

(Erase heading not required.)

Place	Date	Hour	Summary of Events and Information	Remarks and references to Appendices
PESELHOEK	1916 June 18		Capt. F.C. ROSS-BROWN R.F.A. appointed Adjutant 90th Brigade R.F.A. Capt. H.P. BERESFORD-POER. R.F.A. from 89⁰ Battery to command No.1 Section. DAB. No.4 Section had a G.S. Wagon destroyed by shell fire at St. JEAN near YPRES. DAB	
	19		A Gunner of No.1 Section died of wounds. DAB	
			Lt. B.G. TWYCROSS R.F.A. posted from No.3 Section to 91st Brigade. DAB	
	20		Lt. Col. J.R. FOSTER, R.A. having returned from leave resumes command of the Column. DAB	
			Lt. W.T. HILL, R.F.A. to command No.1 Section during absence on leave of Capt. BERESFORD-POER, R.F.A.	
	24		2nd Lt. A.W. KERBY, R.F.A. proceeded on 7 days leave. DAB	
	25		A Court of Inquiry was held to inquire into the loss of a G.S. Wagon by No.2 Section on the 13th June - finding - No blame attaching to No.2 Section and loss chargeable to the public. DAB	

Confidential

WAR DIARY
20th Div. Amm. Col. R.F.A.   Army Form C. 2118.

INTELLIGENCE SUMMARY.   JUNE. 1916.

(Erase heading not required.)

33

Place	Date	Hour	Summary of Events and Information	Remarks and references to Appendices
	1916			
PESELHOEK	June 27		No. 4 Section had the following casualties near YPRES whilst employed on R.E. fatigues :- 1 man killed - 3 men wounded. 2 drivers severely wounded - all by shell fire. AAA 1 wagon badly damaged. AAA No. 4 Section had one man wounded whilst attached to D/93 Battery. AAA	
	29		No. 4 Section had 3 men wounded whilst attached to D/93 Battery. AAA Capt. H.P. BERESFORD-PEIRSE, R.F.A. assumes Command of No. 1 Section on his return from leave AAA	
	30		Lt. W.T. HILL, R.F.A. to return to No. 2 Section for duty. AAA The ammunition requirements of the Batteries for the month were heavy, and owing to this and the absence of men from the Column for work on OPs etc. the Column was kept at very high pressure for the whole of this period. AAA	

W.Martin Lt. Col. R.A.
Comdg. 20th Div. Amm. Col.

WAR DIARY

Divisional Ammunition Column,

20th DIVISION.

J U L Y

1 9 1 6

Confidential

War Diary 28th Div. Amm. Col. R.F.A.

Vol 12

WAR DIARY or INTELLIGENCE SUMMARY
(Erase heading not required.)

Army Form C. 2118.

July 1916

34

Place	Date	Hour	Summary of Events and Information	Remarks and references to Appendices
PESELHOEK AND WINNITIGNE	1916 July 1		2nd Lt. E.H. SMITH. R.F.A. No. 4 Section is struck off the strength on being invalided to England. 7798.	
	11		A Court of Inquiry was held to enquire into the loss of a J.S. Wagon by No. 4 Section (Reviewed Capt. T.A. CODNER R.F.A.) 7798	
	15		2nd Lt. C.G.L. ROBERTSON R.F.A. resumes command of the Brout Section on his return from Field Ambulance – 2nd Lt. RAWSON R.F.A. consequently returns to No. 1 Section. 7798	
	14		2nd Lt. V.V. FABER, R.F.A. No. 4 Section is struck off the strength on being ordered to return to England and report to War Office. 7798	
	15		2nd Lt. W. MUIR R.F.A. having arrived from 91st Brigade is posted to No. 4 Section. 7798	
	25		All the S.A.A. and Brout Sections of the Column under the command of Lt. W.T. HILL, R.F.A. entrained at BAVINCHOVE (CASSEL) for DOULLENS, en route to join 20th Division. 7798	
	28		2/3 rds of 29th D.A.C. S.A.A. Section arrived and were attached to the corresponding Section of this Column. 7798.	
	26		2nd Lt. E.H.R. PARRELL, R.F.A. having arrived from 93rd Bde. is posted to No. 4 Section. 7798	

Confidential

26th Div. Amm. Col. R.F.A.

Army Form C. 2118.

WAR DIARY
INTELLIGENCE SUMMARY.

July 1916.

35.

(Erase heading not required.)

Instructions regarding War Diaries and Intelligence Summaries are contained in F. S. Regs., Part II. and the Staff Manual respectively. Title pages will be prepared in manuscript.

Place	Date	Hour	Summary of Events and Information	Remarks and references to Appendices
	1916			
PESELHOEK	July 28		Lt. R.G. RUSSELL R.F.A. having returned from Base Details to proceed to No. 3 Section 1795.	
VLAMATINGHE	29		The remaining 1/3rd of S.A.A. Subsections of 29th D.A.C. arrived. 3 Officers in all arrived from 29th D.A.C. as follows:— 2nd Lts. DALE, MORRIS and RHODES. 1795	

J.M Rhodes Lt Col.
Commdg 26th D.A.C.

20th Divisional Artillery.

20th DIVISIONAL AMMUNITION COLUMN

AUGUST 1 9 1 6

Secret

War Diary

20th Divn D.A.C.

5th to 31st August 1916

(VOLUME) XIV

Staff Captain,
R.A. 20th Division.

Confidential.

Herewith War Diary for
the Column for month of August 1916.

J. Renner
Capt. R.F.A.
Adjt.

for LT. COLONEL R.F.A.
COMMANDING 20th DIVISIONAL AMMUNITION COLUMN.

3/18/18

Confidential

WAR DIARY

or

INTELLIGENCE SUMMARY.

(Erase heading not required.)

Army Form C. 2118.

2nd D.A.C. RFA

August 1916

Place	Date	Hour	Summary of Events and Information	Remarks and references to Appendices
PESELMOER and ILLAVATINGHE	1916 Aug 5		2nd Lt. E.H.R. FARRELL RFA proceeded on 7 days special leave to France to England. JPB	36
	10		Lt. M J HILL RFA to return to Unit of the strength having been ordered to England for instructional purposes. JPB	
			2nd Lt. RICHARDS RFA to take over the command of No 2 Section SAA Section detached (temporarily) JPB	
	13		2nd Lt E.H.R FARRELL RFA reported his return from leave. JPB	
	18		A Field General Court martial assembled at these Headquarters President Major A.E.B Fair RFA for the trial of Gunner Arnold Clinton of the 29th DAC attached 26th DAC JPB	
	20		A Field General Court martial assembled at this Headquarters President Major E M Connolly RFA for the trial of Driver J H New of No 2 Section and of Driver Henry George Knight of the 29th DAC attached 20th DAC JPB	
	27		A Court of Enquiry assembled at No 3 Section - President Captain Beresford-Peirse RFA for the purpose of enquiring into the Co-	

Confidential

Army Form C. 2118.

WAR DIARY 20th DAC. RFA
or
INTELLIGENCE SUMMARY. August 1916

(Erase heading not required.)

Instructions regarding War Diaries and Intelligence Summaries are contained in F. S. Regs., Part II. and the Staff Manual respectively. Title pages will be prepared in manuscript.

Place	Date	Hour	Summary of Events and Information	Remarks and references to Appendices
PESELHOEK & LAMATINGHE	1916 Aug 29		On troops belonging to No 3 Section RFA	
	30		The following Officers took place on the re-organisation of the Brigade of the 2nd Divisional Artillery into 6 gun batteries. Adjutant Capt R.A. DENMAN RFA. Lt. S. REYNOLDS RFA to No 1 Section. Lt. J.E. TATE RFA to No 2 Section. Lt. F.M. BUTLER and 2/Lt H.V.L. COLLINS to No 3 Section. Lt. WAMELLOWS and 2/Lt Mr. TATHAM to No 4 Section. The following Officers of the Column became surplus attached 20th DAC. Captain F.P. BELCHER RFA surplus originant in the Division. Lt. R.G. RUSSELL, 2/Lt. RAWSON, 2/Lt. W.E.G. KICK, 2/Lt W.MUIR, 2 Lt R.K. BRYDON 2/Lt. E.B. LANE, 2/Lt E.H.R. FARRELL RFA.	
	3		The Belgian Interpreter attached to the Column M. PAUL LE BION left and his turn to join the 36th Division. Belgian Interpreter M. FESTOR arrived and was attached to No. 2 Section RFA	Maton 1st Lt Cmdg 20th DAC

WAR DIARY

S.A.A. SECTION, 20TH DIVISION / Army Form C. 2118.

INTELLIGENCE SUMMARY

(Erase heading not required.)

Vol 1

Hour, Date, Place	Summary of Events and Information	Remarks and References to Appendices
1916 August 1st — COUIN	The Section is a portion of the 20th D.A.C. and was formed on July 28th to accompany the 20th Division on the separation of the 20th Divisional Artillery. It consists of 6 officers 260 O.R., 324 horses and mules 49 G.S. and 15 F.G.S. wagons to carry 1,842,000 Rds. 303 "S.A.A." 7800 - Rds Pistol Webley + 8,100 hand grenades. —	
1/16 — COUIN	Besides the supply of S.A.A. which was drawn from 1st to 16th Aug., the Section was occupied during this period in taking engineers material (sand bags, lumber, compressed wood etc.) from COURCELLES to an advanced dump near the trenches and in carrying out sundry Divisional fatigues. —	
17 — BEAUVAL	Marched to BEAUVAL.	
18 — BOISBERGUES	Marched to BOISBERGUES + attached to 6th D.A.C.	
19 — HAVERNAS	Marched to HAVERNAS with 6th D.A.C.	
20 — VACQUEMONT	Marched to VACQUEMONT with 6th D.A.C.	
22. near MEAULTE	Left 6th D.A.C. and marched to F.19.a. (ALBERT map) and a portion of the Section to BOIS CAFET (F.17.d. Central)	
23/31 — Do. —	Section has used exclusively for the supply of ammunition, grenades and flares + rockets. —	

1 Sept 1916.
J H Myers (?) Lt RFA
OC S.A.A. Section 20th Divn.

20th Divisional Artillery.

20th DIVISIONAL AMMUNITION COLUMN

SEPTEMBER 1 9 1 6

20/ Vol 14

CONFIDENTIAL

WAR DIARY

20th Div Ammn Coln.

From Sept 1st 1916 to Sept 30th 1916

VOL

Army Form C. 2118.

WAR DIARY
or
INTELLIGENCE SUMMARY.
(Erase heading not required.)

Instructions regarding War Diaries and Intelligence Summaries are contained in F. S. Regs., Part II. and the Staff Manual respectively. Title pages will be prepared in manuscript.

Place	Date	Hour	Summary of Events and Information	Remarks and references to Appendices
PESELHOEK	1-7-9-16	9 pm	Weather unsettled all period	PUS - PUS
"	7-9-16	—		PUS
"	8-9-16	10 am	Hunter Brie 20 × Div HQ Command Marred to the SOMME to join the remainder of the Division. 1st DAC, Marched to ZERMEZEELE	PUS
ZERMEZEELE	—	4:30 pm	Arrived & billetted for the night	PUS
"	9-9-16	9 am	Weather fine. Staff Capt. ZERMEZEELE and Marched to REBECQ	PUS
REBECQ	"	4:30 pm	Arrived & billetted in the Village & Bois. when Marched to	PUS
"	10-9-16	8:30 am	Weather unsettled left and Marched to EPS. Roy hop LENS 11	PUS
EPS	10-9-16	5:30 pm	Arrived & billetted for the Night	PUS
"	11-9-16	9 am	Left & marched to MONCHEL Weather unsettled	PUS
MONCHEL	11-9-16	2 pm	Arrived & billeted for the night	PUS
"	12-9-16	9 am	Left & marched to Le Maillard Weather unsettled	PUS
Le Maillard	12-9-16	3 pm	Arrived & billetted for the night	PUS
"	13-9-16	11 am	Left & marched to NAOURS Weather unsettled	PUS
NAOURS	13-9-16	6:30 pm	Arrived & billetted for the night	PUS
"	14-9-16	5:30 am	Left and marched to Rumours above the PUS Bois des TAILLES 2 miles West	PUS

WAR DIARY or INTELLIGENCE SUMMARY

Army Form C. 2118.

Place	Date	Hour	Summary of Events and Information	Remarks and references to Appendices
B.o.S.d.I.M.T.	14.9.16		8th Divl Arty joined the Reserve of IV Army Div XIV	PWS
"	15.9.16	9 pm	Corps Arty in IV Army. - HQ near AMIENS 17 Wealth fine	PWS
			Weather fine. No 4 section arrived in 8 MG ? Arm 2 to XIV Corps area. Engaged	PWS
			in training in the Vicinity of GUÉDECOURT – FLERS – LES BOEUFS	PWS
"	16.9.16	9 pm	Weather fine. No 1R & other ranks arrived. 5 + O.R. reinforcements arrived from Base	PWS
"	17.9.16	9 pm	Weather fine " " " "	PWS
"	18.9.16	9 pm	Weather very wet " " " "	PWS
"	19.9.16	9.30 am	Marching orders received from 20th Div Arty 2 Dr Ammn. No 2 section marched to morning rdvs	PWS
			CARNOY to be attached to Guards D.A.C. 92nd Bde R.F.A. having been sent to Guards Div	
			to army them. Weather stormy unsettled.	
"	20.9.16	8 pm	Marching orders rec'd from 20th R.F.A. 2nd to No 3 Section Marched to morning near CARNOY to	PWS
			be attached to Guards D.A.C. 95th Bde R.F.A. having been sent to Guards to train with them	PWS
			Weather unsettled Stormy	PWS
"	21.9.16	9 pm	Weather fine & dry dewey	PWS
"	22.9.16	8 am	No 1 Sect. under orders rec'd from 20 Div R.A. 26 Divl marched to morning near CARNOY to	PWS
			be attached to 61st D.A.C. supply Ammn to 91st Bde in action North of COMBLES	

WAR DIARY
INTELLIGENCE SUMMARY

Army Form C. 2118.

Place	Date	Hour	Summary of Events and Information	Remarks and references to Appendices
BOIS de TAILLES	23.9.16	9pm	Weather fine. No patrols gone out tonight.	
"	24.9.16	9pm	" " " " "	
"	25.9.16	9pm	" " " " "	
"	26.9.16	9pm	" " " " "	
"	27.9.16	9pm	Wet " " " "	
"	28.9.16	9pm	Unsettled	
"	29.9.16	9.30pm	Weather Wet. Battn. when relieved from "PARA – SQ DMS & ROYAL ave transferred to Brunon about CARNOY to refrom reserves of to DMS and from 12 am on Thistledk Hd DMS became responsible for supply of ammun to 20th & 91st Bdes	
CARNOY	30.9.16	9pm	Weather fine. All available transport in delivery ammun to frontline	

J.M. Denman Capt. RFA
for

20th Divisional Artillery.

20th DIVISIONAL AMMUNITION COLUMN

OCTOBER 1 9 1 6

Vol 13

CONFIDENTIAL

War Diary.

of

20th Divisional Ammunition Column
R.F.A.

from 1st October 1916   to   31st October 1916

Confidential

Staff Captain
R.A. 20th Division

[Stamp: 20th DIVISIONAL AMMUNITION COLUMN No. R2500 Date........ R.F.A.]

Herewith War Diary
for month of October 1916
for this Column.

31·10·16.

F H Dennis Capt. R.F.A.
Adjutant for
LT. COLONEL R.F.A.
COMMANDING 20th DIVISIONAL AMMUNITION COLUMN

WAR DIARY
INTELLIGENCE SUMMARY.

(Erase heading not required.)

Army Form C. 2118.

(By Map Carnoy 57ed sheet ALBERT)

Place	Date	Hour	Summary of Events and Information	Remarks and references to Appendices
CARNOY	1-10-16	9 p.m.	Heather fine. Nothing of military to note.	F.JNS.
"	2-10-16	9 p.m.	Heather fine. Amm. Dump opened at F12c	F.JNS.
"	3-10-16	9 p.m.	Heather wet. Amm. Transport very difficult owing to state of roads & heavy local rain	F.JNR. F.JNS.
"	4-10-16	9 p.m.	Heather wet. Emergency Parks made with Amm. O.K. Talks from Amm. Wag. & Amm. Supply.	F.JNS.
"	5-10-16	9 p.m.	Ammunition Park chiefly by pack animals. 4/5 O.R. prs. to Btys as reinforcements from the Res.	F.JNR. G.JNS.
"	6-10-16	9 p.m.	Heather wet. Pack animal deliveries very doubtful & supply continued in this manner.	S.JNR.
"	7-10-16	9 p.m.	Heather wet. Nothing to note.	F.JNS.
"	8-10-16	9 p.m.	" " " "	" - opened to 9.15 pm
"	9-10-16	9 p.m.	Heather dull 2+ hr. rain. Amm. Dump at F12c closed out a forward dump opened at BRICQUETRIE A4.8.3.0. 44 O.R. & 2 r k Brs. as reinforcements.	F.JNR.
"	10-10-16	9 p.m.	Heather dull. Nothing of importance.	F.JNS.
"	11-10-16	9 p.m.	" " " sent some 3 Amm. by tram to Guillemont Station from whence it was delivered by pack animals to Batteries - night to Antoine	F.JNS.
"	12-10-16	9 p.m.	Heather dull. Nothing to note. 53 O.R. reinforcements arrived from Base Depot.	F.JNS.

WAR DIARY or INTELLIGENCE SUMMARY

Army Form C. 2118.

Place	Date	Hour	Summary of Events and Information	Remarks and references to Appendices
CARNOY	13.10.16	9am	Weather fine but dull. Marched to hut F.34.D.O.R. dist. to R/Ms. arrived for Base depot & reinforcements	Pte.
"	15.10.16	"	Weather fine. Colr. Commenced work on dump at MARICOURT dug out.	Pte.
"	16.10.16	"	New dump from above Run — to be up by G.S. Wgn. to Divn. dump. Arb.30 BRIQUETERIE R? 31.O.R sent 15 R/Ms as reinforcements	Pte.
"	17.10.16	"	Weather wet. R/Ms to A.C.	Pte.
"	18.10.16	"	"	Pte.
"	19.10.16	"	"	Pte.
"	20.10.16	"	10.O.R reinforcements arrived from Base Depot	Pte.
"	21.10.16	"	10.O.R. sent to R/Ms reinforcements	Pte.
"	23.10.16	"	4.O.R arrived from Base depot reinforcements & posted to 91/92 R/Ms	Pte.
"	25.10.16	"	20 - O.R. reinforcements arrived from Base Depot	Pte.
"	26.10.16	"	30 - O.R " " posted from Col to R/Ms	Pte.
"	27.10.16	"	14 - O.R " " arrived from Base Depot	Pte.
"	"	"	17 - O.R " " posted to R/Ms from this Col	Pte.
"	30.10.16	"	Weather unsettled - wet. Jas. O.R. sect No 4 section placed on disposal	Pte.
"	31.10.16	"	Marched to BERNAFAY WOOD. Weather unsettled. Park to unto	F.T.

LN Foster PAdj
Comdg 20th D.A.C.

20th Divisional Artillery

20th DIVISIONAL AMMUNITION COLUMN

NOVEMBER 1 9 1 6

Vol 16

WAR DIARY

FOR

Nov 1st to 30th 1916

20th Divisional Ammunition Column

Bde Major.
R.A. 20th Division.   Confidential

Herewith War Diary
for the 20th Divl. Ammn Column
R.F.A. for the present month.

A.J. Sullivan Lt. R.F.A.
adjt.

29/11/½
for LT. COLONEL R.F.A.
COMMANDING 20th DIVISIONAL AMMUNITION COLUMN.

20th Div. Amm. Col. R.F.A.

Army Form C. 2118.

WAR DIARY
for Nov. 1916.
INTELLIGENCE SUMMARY.

Map Ref. — ALBERT
combined sheet

Place	Date	Hour	Summary of Events and Information	Remarks and references to Appendices
CARNOY	1/11/16		13 O.R. Reinforcements posted to Brigades, and 38 received from Base Depot	attd
"	2/11/16		30 " " " " "	attd
"	3/11/16 to 5/11/16		nothing to report; no reinforcements sent to Brigades	attd
"	6/11/16		2/Lt. P.W. Hamilton arrived from 2nd Reserve R.F.A. Brigade.	attd
"	7/11/16 to 14/11/16		Nothing unusual to report: 20 Reinforcements, including N.Co's artificers arrived from Base Depot and reposted to Brigades	attd
"	14/11/16 to 19/11/16		Leave reopens: but is cancelled a few days later. 40 Reinforcements, including Sergeant, m, and telephonists arrived and reposted to Brigades	attd
"	20/11/16 to 24/11/16		20 Reinforcements arrive, and are reposted to Brigades. Leave reopens. D.A.C. send party of 7 all ranks; increases later to 12.	attd
"	25/11/16	noon	4th D.A.C. Dumps at the PLATEAU is taken over from by the D.A.C.	attd
"	26/11/16		20th D.A.C. Dumps at GUILLEMONT, MARICOURT STONE-SIDING, and at THE BRICQUETERIE, (BERNAFAY WOOD ROAD — A 4.b. 3.0) to 2nd AUSTRALIAN DIVISION. All fatigues for the XIV Corps ceased on this date	attd

E.W.Walker Col.R.F.A.

WAR DIARY

INTELLIGENCE SUMMARY

Army Form C. 2118.

Page 2.

Place	Date	Hour	Summary of Events and Information	Remarks and references to Appendices
CARNOY	26/4/16 (contd)		No. 1 Section left their camp 3.0 a.m. and proceeded with R.F.A. H.Q 1s and 91st Bde R.F.A. to rest area, halting at CORBIE for the night. Remainder of the Column became attached to the 8th Divisional Artillery. S.A.C. takes over the R.E. dump of the 20th Divisional Artillery. Lt. Col. Foster proceeds on leave and Column is commanded by Capt. Walker.	atd
"	28/4/16		Administration of the Column is changed to the 17th Divisional Artillery, this formation relieving the 8th Divl Artillery.	atd
"	29/4/16		The S.A.A. Section of the 29th D.A.C. is relieved by the Column, each Section of the Column sending part of their Small Arms Sub-Section.	atd
"	22/4/16		The S.A.A. Section of the Column at BERNAFAY WOOD is relieved by 5th Australian Division. No. 1 Section on this.	atd
"	26/4/16		No. 3 Section move into camp later occupied by No. 1 Section proceeding to rest area. No. 4 Section move into camps lately occupied by B/91. Bde R.F.A and D/91. Bde R.F.A, at square F.18.n. ("Albert" Combined Sheet).	atd

Ewell McCay Capt R.F.A.
Commdg. 20 th D.A.C. R.F.A.

20th Divisional Artillery

20th DIVISIONAL AMMUNITION COLUMN

DECEMBER 1 9 1 6

Vol 17

Confidential.

War Diary

December 1916.

(Original Copy)

20th Divisional Ammn. Column. R.F.A WAR DIARY

Army Form C. 2118.

INTELLIGENCE SUMMARY

December 1916.

Place	Date	Hour	Summary of Events and Information	Remarks and references to Appendices
"F.17.d.4.9." Combined Rail. "Meaulte"	Dec 1st	—	19 other ranks reinforcements arrive, and posted to Sections (including 6 telephonists)	R.N.S.
	4th	—	(a) 4 Officers (2nd Lieuts.) arrived — posted later to Brigades R.F.A. (b) 2/Lieut. A.J. MORRIS (on appointment to permanent commission from 71st Bde R.F.A.) arrived, and posted to No 3 Section.	R.N.S. R.N.S.
	5th	—	49 other ranks posted to Brigades R.F.A. as reinforcements.	R.N.S.
	10th	—	Administration of the Column returns to 20th Divisional Artillery (Brig. General Browell C.M.G.) — from 17th Divisional Artillery.	R.N.S.
	11th	—	90 other ranks reinforcements arrive and posted to Sections.	R.N.S.
	13th	—	1 Fitter Corporal and 9 telephonists arrive as reinforcements — posted later to Brigades R.F.A. 10 other ranks reinforcement posted to Bdes R.F.A.	R.N.S.
	19th	—	28 other ranks reinforcements are posted to Brigades R.F.A. from Column.	R.N.S.
	26th	"	Court of Enquiry assembles at No 4 Section to enquire into the circumstances attending the death of a man who died in No 4 Section	R.N.S.

Army Form C. 2118.

20th Div. Amm. Col. R.F.A.

WAR DIARY
INTELLIGENCE SUMMARY
(Erase heading not required.)

December 1916   Page 2

Instructions regarding War Diaries and Intelligence Summaries are contained in F. S. Regs., Part II. and the Staff Manual respectively. Title pages will be prepared in manuscript.

Place	Date	Hour	Summary of Events and Information	Remarks and references to Appendices
	26th	—	Administration of the Column comes under 17th Divisional Artillery on R.A. HQ. 20th Div. moving to CORBIE (Rest area).	P. M̄.
	27th	11 a.m.	Formation of a T.A.A. Section under orders from HQ XIV Corps, made by transferring and exchanging weapon & men trucks from No. 4 Section ("B" Echelon) to Section of "A" Echelon; leaving No. 4 Section as the T.A.A Section – consisting of 1 Captain, 3 Subalterns, 196 other ranks, 248 horses, 30 G.S. wagons and 15 limbered G.S. wagons. Above arrangement purely temporary and local and do not, in any way, interfere with War Establishments.	P. M̄.
	27th	10 a.m.	No. 1 Section leave Rest Billets at MORLANCOURT and takes over camp occupied by No. 3 Section (A.13.d.4.2.)	P. M̄.
		11 a.m.	No. 2 Section leave camp (F.18.c.0.7) and proceed to Rest Billets at MORLANCOURT.	
		11.30 a.m.	No. 3 Section moves into camp previously occupied by No. 2 Section (i.e. F.18.c.0.7)	

"ALBERT" Continued Rest

F. 17. d. 9.9

L.N.Forbes
LT. COLONEL R.F.A.
COMMANDING 20th DIVISIONAL AMMUNITION COLUMN.

Confidential.

War Diary
of
20th Divisional Ammunition Column RFA

January 1917.

(Original Copy)

Army Form C. 2118.

WAR DIARY
or
INTELLIGENCE SUMMARY.
(Erase heading not required.)

Unit:- 20th Divisional Ammunition Column R.F.A.

Month:- January 1917

Instructions regarding War Diaries and Intelligence Summaries are contained in F. S. Regs., Part II. and the Staff Manual respectively. Title pages will be prepared in manuscript.

Place	Date	Hour	Summary of Events and Information	Remarks and references to Appendices
	2nd	—	2/Lieut. H. Payne-McLuen is appointed Divisional Grenade Officer vice 2/Lieut. H.G. W. Godfrey who rejoins No. 4 Section, 20th D.A.C.	RWS
	4th	—	41 Other ranks posted to Brigades R.F.A. as reinforcements. 11 Other ranks arrived from Base depôt as reinforcements.	RWS
	7th	—	5 Staff Sergeants and Sergeants posted to Brigade as reinforcements. 29 Other ranks arrived from Base Depôt as reinforcements.	RWS
	12th	—	Reorganization commences i.e. No. 3 Section leaves Divisional Ammunition Column and becomes "93rd" Brigade Ammunition Column." Consequent upon reorganization Column to Army Field Artillery Brigade. The establishment of Sections of Echelon "A" is increased and that of Echelon "B" slightly diminished. Deficiencies in Sections of Echelon "A" (i.e. Nos 1 and 2 Sections) are made up from No 3 Section before their departure to Reserve Area. No 2 Section return to the line from Rest Area, and occupy camp vacated by No. 3 Section (i.e. F.18.c.0.7). No 4 Section cease to act as "S.A.A. Section" to the Division.	RWS

(ALBERT – Bouzincourt Road)
F 17 d. 9.9.

20th D.A.C. R.F.A.   WAR DIARY   Army Form C. 2118.
(continuation INTELLIGENCE SUMMARY   Page 2

Place	Date	Hour	Summary of Events and Information	Remarks and references to Appendices
	19th	—	12 other ranks arrived from Base Depot as Reinforcements	PJF
	20th	—	The 15 hirelings – G.S. before held in charge by the Column are exchanged for a corresponding number of S.A.A. Carts from the GUARDS division. 30 other ranks are posted to Brigades as reinforcements.	PJF
	22nd		2/Lt. E. BARKER (S.R.) having arrived from 30th D.A.C. is posted to N°2 Section in exchange for 2/Lt. F. COATES who rejoins 30th D.A.C. on return from leave.	PJF
	29th		B.S.M. (W.O Cl II) f/is [?] listed on appointment to permanent Commission is posted to GUARDS Divisional Artillery on 2/[?].	PJF

W.N Foster
LT. COLONEL R.F.A.
COMMANDING 20th DIVISIONAL AMMUNITION COLUMN.

Vol 19

Confidential
War Diary

20th Div. Amm. Col.

Army Form C. 2118.

20th Divisional Ammunition Column R.F.A.   Month

WAR DIARY
or
INTELLIGENCE SUMMARY.   February 1917.
(Erase heading not required.)

Instructions regarding War Diaries and Intelligence
Summaries are contained in F. S. Regs., Part II.
and the Staff Manual respectively. Title pages
will be prepared in manuscript.

Place	Date	Hour	Summary of Events and Information	Remarks and references to Appendices
(ALBERT – continued sheet)	3rd	—	2/Lieut. M.C.H. Clarkson arrived from 2/B/9/26 battery R.F.A., was taken on the strength of the Column and posted to No. 4 Section	R/JKS
	7th	—	Leave was re-opened.	R.Mt. R/JKS
	9th	—	Leave again suspended.	R/JKS
	11th	—	A Field General Court Martial assembled for the trial of B.Q.M.S. Andrews W. and afterbarded (Rules 29 book of) No.1 Section	R/JKS
	2/Lieut. S.W. Awdrey having reported his arrival from R.H. and R.F.A. Base Depot was temporarily attached to the Column by authority of G.O.C., R.A. 20th Division.		R/JKS
	17th	—	177 other ranks arrived from R.H. and R.F.A. Base Depot and were distributed amongst the Sections of the Column	R/JKS
	18th	—	103 other ranks reinforcements were sent to Brigades and Divl. Trench Mortars	R/JKS

Army Form C. 2118.

(Continued).

WAR DIARY
or
INTELLIGENCE SUMMARY.

(Erase heading not required.)

Place	Date	Hour	Summary of Events and Information	Remarks and references to Appendices
	21st	—	4 N.C.O's of the Column were sent to an Instructional Course on defensive measures against gas attacks.	F.M.S.
	22nd	—	24 other ranks arrived from R.H. and R.F.A. Base Depot and were distributed amongst the Sections of the Column.	R.M.S.
	23rd	—	24 other ranks reinforcements were sent to Brigades.	R.M.S.
	25th	—	A Field General Court Martial assembled for the trial of Corporal Tiley A/91st Brigade R.F.A. This court was adjourned.	R.M.S.
	26th	—	2/Sgt. C.V. Rich departed to report in London for a cadet school with a view to training as an Officer. Lieut. Colonel J.N. Forbes R.F.A. proceeded on ten days leave of absence to BIARRITZ and Captain T.A. Coeur R.F.A. No. 2 Section assumed command of the Column.	R.M.S.
	27th	—	R.Q.M.S. Palmgren F.A. departed to report in London for a cadet school with a view to training as an Officer.	R.M.S.

WAR DIARY
or
INTELLIGENCE SUMMARY.

(Erase heading not required.)

Army Form C. 2118.

Place	Date	Hour	Summary of Events and Information	Remarks and references to Appendices
	27th		A Field General Court Martial assembled for the trial of Driver Thwaites A. No.1 Section and of Driver Jacobs S. B/92nd Brigade R.F.A.	Appx

J.H. Denman
Capt. R.A.
Adjutant B. Bde.
for O.C.

Vol 20
/

Confidential

War Diary

20th Divnl.

Ammntn. Column.

March 1917

WAR DIARY 20 Div Amm Colm

or

INTELLIGENCE SUMMARY.

(Erase heading not required.)

Army Form C. 2118.

March 1917

Date	Hour	Summary of Events and Information	Remarks and references to Appendices
1st.		The Column took over charge of the GUILLEMONT dump from 17th Divisional Artillery and 2/Lieut. F.F. WYER R.F.A. was put in charge.	
3rd		A Field General Court Martial assembled at this Column's Headquarters for the trial of No. 64018 Corporal Tilley C of "A" Battery, 91st Brigade R.F.A.	
5th		The Column assumed control of the CARNOY watering point and fatigue parties being provided by Brigades and Divisional Trench Mortars, the watering point was kept in thorough working order, measures taken to avoid undue congestion.	
7th		Capt. N.S. McINTYRE (Church of England Chaplain to the Forces) having completed his contract departed for England from attached 20th D.A.C.	

WAR DIARY
INTELLIGENCE SUMMARY

Army Form C. 2118.

Place	Date	Hour	Summary of Events and Information	Remarks and references to Appendices
	7th		Capt. D.E. WALL RAMC having rejoined from sick leave of absence reassumes medical charge of 20th D.A.C. vice Capt. H.S. MULLAN RAMC who rejoined 60th Field Ambulance (authority A.D.M.S. 20th Division).	
	9th		Lieut. Colonel J.R. FOSTER R.F.A. having rejoined from leave of absence reassumes command of the Column vice Capt. T.A. CODNER R.F.A. who reassumes command of his (No. 2) Section.	
	15th		The Small Arms Ammunition Section (No. 3 Section) commanded by Capt. W. LAING R.F.A. completed to establishment of ammunition concentrated in or about TRONES WOOD & constructed three separate dumps of ammunition in the vicinity. On this date the Small Arms Ammunition Section passed out of the control of Officer Commanding, 20th D.A.C. & came under the direct orders of "Q" Office 20th Division.	

WAR DIARY
or
INTELLIGENCE SUMMARY.
(Erase heading not required.)

Army Form C. 2118.

Place	Date	Hour	Summary of Events and Information	Remarks and references to Appendices
	19th		The Column took over charge of the COMBLES dump (ammunition) from 29th Divisional Artillery and 2/Lieut. E.W. AUSTIN RFA was put in charge.	RMK
	20th		2/Lieut. E. BARKER RFA. relieved 2/Lieut. F.F. WYER RFA at the GUILLEMONT dump and the latter officer returned to his (No.1) Section. Two men of the Column were detailed to attend a beginners signalling course in CARNOY camps.	RMK
	21st		Headquarters and the "A" Echelon (comprising No.1 and 2 Sections) moved forward to camps in the locality of LEUZE WOOD.	RHK
	27th		2/Lieut. BARRETT RFA (Divisional Trench Mortars) with party of 20 men moved forward re-established an ammunition dump at BUS.	RK

Army Form C. 2118.

WAR DIARY

or

~~INTELLIGENCE SUMMARY~~

(Erase heading not required.)

Place	Date	Hour	Summary of Events and Information	Remarks and references to Appendices
			On the 25th March 1917 at 2pm the 20th Divisional Ammunition Column RFA. as a unit of the 20th Division passed from the control of the XIVth to the XVIIth Corps. During the whole month particular attention was paid to salvage work. Special efforts were made with the assistance of three officers of Divisional Trench Mortars, fatigue parties were organised and a systematic clearance was effected from the forward area & vacated battery positions, of all kinds of ammunition empties.)	

J.H. Brennan
Capt RFA
for
LT. COLONEL R.F.A.
COMMANDING 20th DIVISIONAL AMMUNITION COLUMN.

Confidential Vol 21

War Diary
of
20th Divnl. Ammunition Column. RFA
from 1st April 1917 to 30th April 1917.

WAR DIARY
or
INTELLIGENCE SUMMARY.
(Erase heading not required.)

Army Form C. 2118.

Place	Date	Hour	Summary of Events and Information	Remarks and references to Appendices
LEUZE WOOD.	1st		128 remounts were collected from CERISY and distributed proportionally amongst batteries and Sections of the Column. 27 reinforcements were sent to Brigades of 20th Divisional Artillery.	PMS
	3rd		Capt. R.H. DENMAN, RFA (Adjutant) proceeded on 10 days leave to England and 2/Lieut. P.W. HAMILTON RFA assumed duties of Adjutant.	PMS
	6th		2/Lieut. E. BARKER, RFA of No. 2 Section relieved 2/Lt K.G. BARRETT RFA (Divisional Trench Mortars) as Officer in charge BUS ammunition dump, and the last named Officer rejoined his own unit.	PMS
	7th		28 other rank reinforcements joined the Column from R.H. & R.F.A. Base Depot, Havre.	PMS
	8th		A fatigue party under the supervision of 2/Lieut. E.W AUSTIN RFA attended at the COMBLES ammunition dump to sort & stack for removal the ammunition at that dump.	PMS

Army Form C. 2118.

WAR DIARY
or
INTELLIGENCE SUMMARY.
(Erase heading not required.)

Instructions regarding War Diaries and Intelligence Summaries are contained in F. S. Regs., Part II. and the Staff Manual respectively. Title pages will be prepared in manuscript.

Place	Date	Hour	Summary of Events and Information	Remarks and references to Appendices
LEUZE WOOD	8th		Capt. H.B.POER R.F.A commanding No.1 Section proceeded on 10 days leave to England and 2/Lieut H.MAYNARD, R.F.A. assumed temporary command of No.1 Section during his absence.	F.M.S.
	9th		2/Lieut. C.E.BURRIDGE, 13th Reserve Regt. of Cavalry joined the Column in the capacity of Adviser in Horsemanship. (Authority 3rd Army AE/7110 of — 2/3/17)	F.M.S.
	11th		16 reinforcements were sent to 15 Brigades of 20th Divisional Artillery.	F.M.S.
	13th		2/Lieut. C.E.BURRIDGE (above mentioned) was posted to 6th Corps (Authority XVth Corps, C.S.C./160 of — 11/4/17). 12 reinforcements were sent to 15 Brigades of 20th Divisional Artillery.	F.M.S.
	17th		Headquarters and "A" Echelon moved forward to BUS (map refce. O 24 central, Map of France, Sheet 57c (1/40000)	F.M.S.

1577 Wt. W10791/1773 500,000 1/15 D. D. & L. A.D.S.S./Forms/C. 2118.

WAR DIARY
or
INTELLIGENCE SUMMARY.
(Erase heading not required.)

Army Form C. 2118.

Place	Date	Hour	Summary of Events and Information	Remarks and references to Appendices
B U S	18th		Capt. R.H. DENMAN, R.F.A. having returned from leave resumed the duties of Adjutant and 2/Lt. P.W. HAMILTON, R.F.A. returns to his (No.1) Section and takes over temporary command from 2/Lt. H. MAYNARD, R.F.A.	P/Sgt S
	20th		2/Lieut. E.K.W. THOMPSON, R.F.A. was posted to join the Colonel from Guards Divisional Artillery but remained detached on special duty under Corps arrangements. 2/Lieut. H.G.W. GODFREY, R.F.A. No. 3 Section was posted to 92nd Brigade, R.F.A.	P/Sgt S
	21st		2/Lieut. H. MAYNARD, R.F.A. No. 1 Section proceeded on 10 days leave to England.	P/Sgt S
	22nd		Capt. H.B. POER, R.F.A. having returned from leave resumed command of his (No.1) Section.	P/Sgt S

WAR DIARY
or
INTELLIGENCE SUMMARY

Army Form C. 2118.

Place	Date	Hour	Summary of Events and Information	Remarks and references to Appendices
BUS	23rd		An ammunition dump was established at NEUVILLE-BOURTONVAL and 2/Lt T.C. HUNTER, R.F.A, of No. 3 Section put in charge. A class was formed to train men as telephonists to replace casualties in batteries and 98054 Corpl. W.G. Powell was posted from D/9/1st battery to the Column as N.C.O. Instructor in charge of this class.	P.H.S
	26th		A Board of Officers comprising Capt. G. SIMONS, A.V.C. President and Lt. A. McDONALD, R.F.A. & 2/Lt. W.T. UNMACK, R.F.A. members, assembled, and examined horses out 3 men of the Column as shoeing smiths.	P.H.S
	28th		2/Lieut. F.F. WYER, R.F.A. of No. 1 Section relieved 2/Lieut. T.C. HUNTER, R.F.A. as Officer i/c NEUVILLE ammunition dump and the last named Officer returned to his (No. 3) Section.	P.H.S

Army Form C. 2118.

WAR DIARY
or
INTELLIGENCE SUMMARY.
(Erase heading not required.)

Place	Date	Hour	Summary of Events and Information	Remarks and references to Appendices
			During the latter part of the month the ammunition at COMBLES was gradually cleared, the ammunition being brought forward to BUS. when such clearance was effected 2/Lt. E.W. AUSTIN, R.F.A. was relieved of duty at the dump & returned to his (No.2) Section.	P.K.D.

J.H.Denman Capt R.F.A

Lt. COLONEL R.F.A.
COMMANDING 29th DIVISIONAL AMMUNITION COLUMN.

Confidential Vol 22

War Diary

of

1st May 1917 to 31st May 1917

20th Div. Amm'n Col'n

WAR DIARY
INTELLIGENCE SUMMARY

Army Form C. 2118

Place	Date	Hour	Summary of Events and Information	Remarks and references to Appendices
BUS	1st		After nightfall ammunition was delivered by "A" Echelon to advanced positions of gun Brigade R.F.A in & about METZ-EN-COUTURE (map reference Q19 & 20).	R.W.T
	2nd		Ammunition was delivered as on evening of 1st. 29 other rank reinforcements joined from R.H. and R.F.A Base Depot.	R.W.T
	3rd		20 G.S. wagon loads of fixed ammunition was drawn from railhead ROCQUIGNY (O.27 central) & delivered at NEUVILLE ammunition dump (P.22.B.5.0).	R.W.T
	4th		34 G.S. wagons } of fixed ammunition was drawn from	R.W.T
	5th		33 G.S. wagons } ROCQUIGNY railhead & delivered at NEUVILLE dump.	R.W.T
	5th		1000 rounds "A" ammunition was transferred from 20th D.A.C. dump NEUVILLE to 40th P.A.C. at FINS (V.12 central).	R.W.T
	6th		31 other rank reinforcements were sent to Brigades of 20th Divisional Artillery.	R.W.T

Army Form C. 2118.

WAR DIARY
or
INTELLIGENCE SUMMARY.
(Erase heading not required.)

Instructions regarding War Diaries and Intelligence Summaries are contained in F. S. Regs., Part II. and the Staff Manual respectively. Title pages will be prepared in manuscript.

Place	Date	Hour	Summary of Events and Information	Remarks and references to Appendices
	7th		4000 rounds "A" ammunition received by lorries taken in charge at NEUVILLE ammunition dump.	R.H.S.
	8th		About 700 rounds 4.5 How. ammunition left by D/92nd Battery in advanced temporary position at Q.28.c.1.4. was collected & dumped at another position at P.11.B.1.6.	R.H.S.
	11th		NEUVILLE ammunition dump was cleared of empty shell cases, which were taken to NOEUX QUIGNY railhead.	R.H.S.
	14th		G.O.C. 20th Division inspected Section camps, mess, animals, turn out, cookhouses, latrines etc., expressed himself quite satisfied.	R.H.S.
	"	9 p.m.	Eight 4.5 How. wagons & teams assisted D/92nd Battery to remove ammunition from P.11.B.1.6. to a new position. 38 other ranks joined from R.H. & H.A. Base Depot (reinforcements) 18 – do – reinforcements were sent to Brigades of 20th Divisional Artillery.	R.H.S.

WAR DIARY
or
INTELLIGENCE SUMMARY.

Army Form C. 2118.

Place	Date	Hour	Summary of Events and Information	Remarks and references to Appendices
	16th	11am	A Field General Court Martial assembled at D.A.C. HQ. for trial of No. 42503 Gr. Leeson W. R.G.A. of 2/20 battery 20th R.A. Trench Mortars.	P.T.S
	18th		NEUVILLE ammunition dump was cleared of empty shell cases which were taken to ROCQUIGNY railhead. All howitzer wagons of the "A" Echelon filled at BUS dump in preparation for expected relief move.	P.T.S.
	19th		All 18pdr. wagons of the "A" Echelon filled at NEUVILLE dump.	P.T.S
	20th and 21st 20th		9.2" & 6" Brigade ammunition wagons were filled to establishment at NEUVILLE dump. All local ammunition in G.S. wagons was taken forward & dumped at H.17.c.5.5 (2nd Australian D.A.C.) to await arrival of this Column.	P.T.S P.T. P.T.S
	23rd 24th		Our G.S. wagons gave to await arrival of 20th Column. All available G.S. wagons were loaned to units of 20th Divisional Artillery to assist them to move.	P.T.S.

WAR DIARY
INTELLIGENCE SUMMARY

Army Form C. 2118.

Place	Date	Hour	Summary of Events and Information	Remarks and references to Appendices
	25th	8.30am	H.Q. and "A" Echelon moved from BUS into new camps about N.24.B.	PArS
	28 Oct	12.30pm	Ammunition dump at I.1.b.3.3 (sheet 57c) was taken over from 2nd Australian D.A.C. & 2 wheit. E. BARKER put in charge. A rear dump at H.19.A.8.2 was also taken over from above unit.	PArS
	30th		H.Q. and "A" Echelon moved forward to camps about H.22.B.	PSrS
	31st		Ammunition dump at VAULX (I.12.3.3) was cleared of supplies which were carted by wagon to railhead about H.21.A.	PArS
			During the month administration of 20th Division (of which 20th Divisional Ammunition Column is a unit) passed from Fourth Army, XVth Corps to Fifth Army, IV Corps.	PArS

F.H. Brennan Capt. R.F.A.
for
Lt. Colonel R.F.A.
20th DIVISIONAL AMMUNITION COL.

WAR DIARY Vol 23
20th Divisional Ammunition
Column.
From 1st June to 30th June 1917

~~MISCELLANEOUS~~

W. 15517—M. 141. 250,000. 1/16. L.S.&Co. Forms/W 3091/2.   Army Form W. 3091.

Cover for Documents.

Nature of Enclosures.

Notes, or Letters written.

WAR DIARY
or
INTELLIGENCE SUMMARY.

(Erase heading not required.)

Army Form C. 2118.

Place	Date	Hour	Summary of Events and Information	Remarks and references to Appendices
Camp near FAVREUIL	2nd		A quantity of German trench mortar bombs on the VAULX-NOREUIL road were salved & taken to ammunition railhead.	R.W.D.
	3rd		Pit props and camouflaged gun covers were drawn from R.E. dumps and delivered to battery positions.	R.W.D.
			12 other rank reinforcements were posted to 20th Divisional Artillery Trench Mortars.	R.W.D.
	4th		Battery positions were cleared of empties which were taken to VAULX ammunition dump.	R.W.D.
	5th		Construction of sandbag walls at VAULX ammunition dump was commenced for protection of ammunition stored there.	R.W.D.
	6th		All trench mortar bombs were removed from VAULX dump to new dump at BEUGNATRE.	R.W.D.
	7th		A quantity of gas & smoke shell arrived & was unloaded and stored on the BEUGNATRE dump. Arrangements were made for guard & police to take charge of R.A. watering troughs near BEUGNATRE.	R.W.D.

Map reference H 22 B
Map of France Sheet 57 c.

Army Form C. 2118.

WAR DIARY
or
INTELLIGENCE SUMMARY.

(Erase heading not required.)

Place	Date	Hour	Summary of Events and Information	Remarks and references to Appendices
	7th		No. 3 Section (Small Arms Section) ceased to be administered by 20th Division "Q" came under direct control of O.C., D.A.C.	D.A.D.S.T.
	8th		36 G.S. wagons were turned out on Divisional fatigues.	D.A.D.S.T.
	9th		35 do	D.A.D.S.T.
	10th		26 do	D.A.D.S.T.
	11th		33 do	D.A.D.S.T.
			Ammunition was delivered to D/91st battery.	D.A.D.S.T.
	12th		28 G.S. wagons were turned out on Divisional fatigues.	D.A.D.S.T.
	13th		31 do	D.A.D.S.T.
			Ammunition was delivered to D/91st battery.	D.A.D.S.T.
	14th		44 G.S. wagons were turned out on Divisional fatigues. 1600 empties were salved & taken to VAULX dump. 4 other tank new/ornaments were posted 20th Divisional Artillery Trench Mortars.	D.A.D.S.T.
	15th		57 G.S. wagons were turned out on Divisional fatigues. Ammunition was delivered to A/91st and D/92nd batteries.	D.A.D.S.T.

WAR DIARY
or
INTELLIGENCE SUMMARY.
(Erase heading not required.)

Army Form C. 2118.

Instructions regarding War Diaries and Intelligence Summaries are contained in F. S. Regs., Part II. and the Staff Manual respectively. Title pages will be prepared in manuscript.

Place	Date	Hour	Summary of Events and Information	Remarks and references to Appendices
	16th		38 G.S. wagons were turned out on Divisional fatigues. Ammunition was delivered to B/91st battery	R.W.S.
	17th		25 G.S. wagons were turned out on Divisional fatigues.	R.W.S.
	18th		38 do	R.W.S.
			Ammunition was delivered to all batteries of 91st Brigade.	R.W.S.
	19th		59 G.S. wagons were turned out on Divisional fatigues.	R.W.S.
	20th		38 do	R.W.S.
	20th and 21st		Echelons of Brigades and D.A.C. were filled up to establishment at VAULX and BEUGNATRE dumps, in preparation for expected relief moving out.	R.W.S.
	21st		2,900 assorted empties collected at dumps & removed to railhead.	R.W.S.
	22nd		13 G.S. wagons were loaned to units of 20th Divisional Artillery for move. Advance parties of 62nd Divl. Artillery took over VAULX and BEUGNATRE dumps, established guards in 20th D.A.C. H.Q. & Section camps.	R.W.S.

WAR DIARY or INTELLIGENCE SUMMARY

Army Form C. 2118.

Place	Date	Hour	Summary of Events and Information	Remarks and references to Appendices
	23rd		H.Q. and A "Echelon" moved back to rest area and occupied camps about X28B (ALBERT map). No. 3 Section remained in old camp & came temporarily under control of "Q" office 20th Division.	R.Ifs
	26th		No. 3 Section moved back to rest area and occupied camps adjoining those of the "A" Echelon.	R.Ifs
	27th		56 recruits arrived & were distributed amongst units of 20th Division.	R.Ifs
	27th to 30th inclusive		This period was occupied by filling deficiencies in all equipment & stores & replacing unserviceable articles. Also by painting all infricted, renumbering up the complete turn out of the Column generally.	R.Ifs

J.H. Denman Capt R.F.A.
for

Confidential

Vol 24

War Diary
of
20ᵗʰ Divi. Ammunt. Col.
1ˢᵗ To 31ˢᵗ July 1917
(Vol 7)

Army Form C. 2118.

WAR DIARY
or
INTELLIGENCE SUMMARY.

(Erase heading not required.)

20th Div. Amm. Column

Instructions regarding War Diaries and Intelligence Summaries are contained in F. S. Regs., Part II. and the Staff Manual respectively. Title pages will be prepared in manuscript.

Place	Date	Hour	Summary of Events and Information	Remarks and references to Appendices
In the field	3rd	6.15am	H.Q. and Sections moved from rest billets in Fauw FRICOURT to camps near MAILLY-MAILLET arriving about 10.30am.	A.R.S.
	4th	11.45am	The Column moved off via BERTRANCOURT, BUS les Artois, AUTHIE arriving at THIEVRES (Map LENS II) about 4pm.	A.R.S.
	5th	9.30am	The Column moved off via HALLOY, LUCHEUX and IVERGNY arriving at CANETTEMONT at 3pm.	A.R.S.
	6th	7am	H.Q. and Nos. 2 and 3 Sections moved off via HOUVIN- HOUVIGNEUL, GOUY en Ternois, and TERNAS arriving at ROELLECOURT at 11am.	A.R.S.
Map LENS II		9am	No.1 Section moved independently under Capt. H.B. POER, R.A. (commanding No.1 section) to billets in RAMECOURT arriving at NOON.	A.R.S.
	7th		This day was spent resting in billets at ROELLECOURT and RAMECOURT respectively and advantage was taken of the halt to make good any defects in vehicles harness and equipment etc.	A.R.S.

WAR DIARY
or
INTELLIGENCE SUMMARY

Army Form C. 2118.

(Erase heading not required.)

Place	Date	Hour	Summary of Events and Information	Remarks and references to Appendices
In the Field	8th	2am	H.Q. and Nos. 2 and 3 Sections left ROELLECOURT having through ST. POL and No. 1 Section joined up in rear of the Column. Column proceeded via VALHUON, TANGRY (Map LENS.11) and FIEFS (Map HAZEBROUCK 5A) to NEDONCHELLE arriving about 6.30am. During this journey a violent storm was experienced, commencing whilst passing through ST. POL with vivid lightning, and very heavy rain the latter of which lasted the whole journey. Despite these adverse climatic conditions a good march was made, the Column arriving at destination well up to time.	A.K.S.
	9th	6am	The Column moved off from NEDONCHELLE via AUCHY-au-Bois, ST. HILAIRE, and AIRE to BOESEGHEM arriving at 10am.	A.K.S.
	10th	5.45am	The Column moved off from BOESEGHEM marching via WALLON CAPPEL occupied billets in the STAPLES area arriving at 9am.	A.K.S.

Map HAZEBROUCK 5A

WAR DIARY
or
INTELLIGENCE SUMMARY.
(Erase heading not required.)

Army Form C. 2118.

Place	Date	Hour	Summary of Events and Information	Remarks and references to Appendices
	11th	6.15am	The Column moved off from the STAPLES area via OXELAERE, and STEENVOORDE and occupied billets south of the STEENVOORDE-POPERINGHE road immediately below BEAUVOORDE WOOD arriving at 9.30am. (i.e. in EECKE area)	P.K.S.
	12th	5.30am	H.Q. and "A" Echelon moved off from the EECKE area via ABEELE and POPERINGHE and occupied camps EAST of the PESELHOEK-WESTVLETEREN Rd in square A14D (Map of Belgium/France Sheet 28) arriving at 8am.	P.K.S.
Map of Belgium and France Sheet 28		9.20am	"B" Echelon left EECKE area marched to HERZEELE in square D9D (Map of Belgium/France Sheet 27) occupied billets established wagon lines near that place.	P.K.S.
	13th		Work was commenced on camps in new area. 19 G.S. wagon loads of ammunition was loaded at 38th D.A.C. dump (A16.A.7.5. Sheet 28) & delivered to batteries of 20th Divisional Artillery	P.K.S.
A14D				

WAR DIARY or INTELLIGENCE SUMMARY

Army Form C. 2118.

Place: Map of Belgium & France Sheet 28 A 14 B 9

Date	Hour	Summary of Events and Information	Remarks and references to Appendices
14th		20 G.S. wagons of ammunition were loaded at 38th D.A.C. dump and delivered to batteries of 20th Divisional Artillery.	Pks
15th		35 G.S. wagons of ammunition were loaded at 38th D.A.C. dump and delivered to batteries of 20th Divisional Artillery.	Pks
16th		6 G.S. wagons and teams of 93rd Field Artillery Brigade Ammunition Column were attached to the Section of "A" Echelon to assist with ammunition fatigues. 40 G.S. wagons of ammunition were loaded at 38th D.A.C. dump and delivered to batteries of 20th Divisional Artillery and 93rd Field Artillery Brigade.	Pks
17th		40 G.S. wagons of ammunition were loaded at 38th D.A.C. dump and delivered to batteries of 20th Divisional Artillery and 93rd Field Artillery Brigade. During delivery of this ammunition, 2 Horsed casualties were sustained, including 2 Officers (2/Lt. F.F. WYER, and 2/Lt. H. GILBERT) wounded, and several other ranks and animals.	Pks

Army Form C. 2118.

WAR DIARY
or
INTELLIGENCE SUMMARY.
(Erase heading not required.)

Place: Map of Belgium & France Sheet 28 A14 D8.9

Date	Hour	Summary of Events and Information	Remarks and references to Appendices
18th		40 G.S. wagons of ammunition were loaded at 38th D.A.C. dump & delivered to batteries of 20th Divisional Artillery and 93rd Field Artillery Brigade.	A/45
19th		3240 HX and 1320 BX ammunition was received by lorry and stored near H.Q. camp under tree cover and camouflaged. 50 G.S. wagons of ammunition was loaded from stock and delivered to batteries of 20th Divisional Artillery and 93rd Field Artillery Brigade.	A/45 A/45
20th		1020 A and 1320 BX ammunition was received by lorry and stored until evening, then loaded into wagons and together with 20 G.S. wagons loaded at 38th D.A.C. dump & delivered to batteries. During delivery casualties other ranks & animals occurred owing to enemy of the enemy.	A/45 A/45

Signed Humphreys Capt. O 35 Div.

WAR DIARY
or
INTELLIGENCE SUMMARY.

(Erase heading not required.)

Army Form C. 2118.

Place	Date	Hour	Summary of Events and Information	Remarks and references to Appendices
Hd of Belgium and France Sheet 28 A 14 D 8 c	20th		3 parties each with NCO/s were detailed for Groups Stations A,C,B, A4A, and A6A, on the Decauville Railway to deal with the ammunition supply of Batteries recorded by these Group Stations at such times as Decauville Rly should be employed.	Pkts
	21st		2000 A, 2000 AX and 1600 BX ammunition arrived by lorry was stored until evening when 26 R.A., 12 Howitzer and 29 G.S. wagons of ammunition were loaded, delivered to batteries. During delivery casualties to other carts and animals were sustained from enemy shell fire.	Pkts.
	22nd		4000 A, 2000 AX and 1000 BX ammunition arrived by lorry was stored until evening, when 33 R.A., 9 Howitzer and 20 G.S. wagons of ammunition were loaded, taken up to batteries of 20th Divisional Artillery whilst on the journey a building and dump were blown up and in sparsely this spot a portion of the convoy was obscured	Pkts

Army Form C. 2118.

WAR DIARY
or
INTELLIGENCE SUMMARY.
(Erase heading not required.)

Instructions regarding War Diaries and Intelligence Summaries are contained in F. S. Regs., Part II. and the Staff Manual respectively. Title pages will be prepared in manuscript.

Place: Map of Belgium and France Sheet 28 A.IV. 9 8 3

Date	Hour	Summary of Events and Information	Remarks and references to Appendices
22nd		& heavily shelled. Severe casualties is killed and wounded other ranks and animals were sustained from shell fire and gas shells, and it proved impossible owing to the road being blocked by dead animals smashed vehicles etc., to deliver part of the ammunition. By means of a fatigue party and several pairs of wheelers the undelivered ammunition was delivered and empty wagons brought back to Sections. 1000 BX ammunition was received by lorry and stored. 18 G.S. and 5 R.A. wagons of ammunition were delivered to batteries of 20th Divisional Artillery.	Appx 1. Appx. Appx.
24th		1440 lethal and 1760 lachrymatory shell were collected from 38th F.A.C. and delivered to Howitzer batteries 20th D. Artillery. 4500 A 4200 AX 2000 BX received by lorry from Corps Ammunition Park and 33 F.A. and 5 G.S. wagon loads of same delivered to batteries of 20th D. Artillery.	Appx.

WAR DIARY
or
~~INTELLIGENCE SUMMARY.~~

(Erase heading not required.)

Army Form C. 2118.

Place	Date	Hour	Summary of Events and Information	Remarks and references to Appendices
	26th		32 R.A. and 51 G.S. wagons of ammunition were delivered from on hand to batteries of 20th Divisional Artillery	Pars PAK.
	26th		3000 A ammunition received from Corps Ammunition Park and 18 R.A. and 9 G.S. wagons ammunition were delivered to batteries.	PAK.
	27th		5000 A and 2000 AX ammunition received from Corps Ammunition Park. Smoke shell was collected from 38th D.A.C. dumps. 17 R.A. and 42 G.S. wagons of ammunition delivered to batteries of 20th Divisional Artillery.	PAK.
	28th		35 R.A. and 15 G.S. wagons of ammunition loaded at 38th DAC dump & from ammunition on hand & delivered to batteries. 11 other rank reinforcements arrived.	PAK.
	29th	10am	No. 3 Section commanded by Capt. W. LAING, R.F.A. marched out and proceeding to the back area came under control of "Q" office 20th Division. Received 2000 AX and 2250 BX from Corps Ammunition Park.	PAK.

WAR DIARY
or
INTELLIGENCE SUMMARY
(Erase heading not required.)

Army Form C. 2118.

Place	Date	Hour	Summary of Events and Information	Remarks and references to Appendices
Huts of Bulgaria & France Sheet 28 A.14 D.8.9	29th		18 B.A. and 11 G.S. wagons ammunition delivered to batteries of 20th Divisional Artillery. 11 other rank reinforcements joined from R.H. and R.F.A. Base Depot.	Appx 5
	30th		Received 2000A 400 BCBR and 800 B/N ammunition from Corps Ammunition Park. 13 G.S. and 10 How. wagons ammunition delivered to batteries of 20th Divisional Artillery, also 20 R.A. wagons in response to an urgent demand.	Appx 5
	31st	9am	Complying with order received in code from Brigade Major 20th Divnl. Artillery J.A.C. H.Q. and "A" Echelon moved forward and camped about B.15 c 8.2 sheet 28.	Appx 5
		7 p.m.	An Officer with party of 2 NCO and 29 men was sent to position about B.17 B 4.4 to establish ammunition dump.	Appx 5
			94 other rank reinforcements joined from R.H. and R.F.A. Base Depot.	Appx 5

WAR DIARY
or
INTELLIGENCE SUMMARY.

Army Form C. 2118.

Place	Date	Hour	Summary of Events and Information	Remarks and references to Appendices
			During the latter half of the month the D.A.C. was called on to work very hard, and during the period 19th to 26th (one week) delivered over 35,000 rounds of gun and howitzer ammunition in addition to returning and resupplying up water to batteries. Also quantities of constructional material and camouflage were supplied, and guns brought out & taken into action. A congratulatory letter from Brig. General W.B. BROWELL C.R.A. 20th Division is attached. The whole of the work carried out as detailed in this diary was in conjunction with XIVth Corps operations against the PILCKEM RIDGE, and the total casualties sustained during the period were 3 officers 37 other ranks and 115 animals, of these 6 other ranks were killed	A/R+S A/R+S A/R+S A/R+S A/R+S

L.V.Eden
Lt. Colonel R.A.
COMMANDING 20th DIVISIONAL AMMUNITION COLUMN

O.C. Divisional Amm: Col"

I wish to place on record my high appreciation of the Excellent work which is being done by the D.A.C. at the present time.

The devotion to duty, under extremely trying circumstances and heavy casualties, the many instances of personal gallantry, many of which are probably unrecorded, and the soldierly determination with which their task has been carried through are worthy of all praise.

I shall be glad if you will convey my appreciation to all ranks, as I wish them to feel that, by their unflinching endurance of the present hard and exhausting conditions, they are worthily carrying on the high traditions not only of the 20th Div! Artillery but of the Royal Regiment as a whole.

(Signed) H.B. Browell
Brig: Gen
C.R.A. 20 Div"

9.7.17

True copy - original attached to forwarded war diary.

Dear Colonel,

I meant to have written before & tell you how much we all appreciate what the SAC have done for us this last fortnight & please tell the Section Commanders also how very sorry we are to hear of all their casualties, & how much we deplore the losses of so many gallant fellows. Hope we may meet soon under more pleasant circumstances & perhaps split another bottle of Pop in Pop.

Yours sincerely
Arthur Erskine

30 July/17

July 29th
My dear Foster

I want to tell you how very much my Brigade appreciates the good work of the D.A.C. during the past fortnight. They have had a very unpleasant time bringing up Ammunition & rations etc ~~& little horse~~ ~~attended to it~~ — both Officers & men have done splendidly. We are indeed proud of our D.A.C. Yours

JHWRicardo

Military Medal.

N.   Sgt   Tooke. E.
. 61896   Sgt   Orr. W
. 69881   Bombr White. W

All the above awards were given in the third battle of YPRES in July & August 1917.

[signature]

Commanding No. 2 Section 20th D.A.C. R.F.A.

CONFIDENTIAL.

WAR DIARY

20TH DIVL AMMN COLN R.F.A.

1ST — 31ST AUGUST 1917.

Vol 25

WAR DIARY
or
INTELLIGENCE SUMMARY.

(Erase heading not required.)

Army Form C. 2118.

Place: B21 B 8 (Corp of Belgium Trench Sheet 28)

Date	Hour	Summary of Events and Information	Remarks and references to Appendices
1st		Ammunition dump was established about B21 B.0.8 (sheet 28) and 2/Lt. E. BARKER RFA placed in charge. This dump worked in conjunction with 38th S.A.C. dump for supply of batteries of 20th and 38th Divisional Artillery	Phot.
2nd		Heavy and continuous rain necessitated the shifting of lorry loads, the ground being of a very marshy nature	Phot.
3rd		Bad weather continued. 40 other rank reinforcements arrived were distributed to units of 20th Divisional Artillery	Phot. Phot.
4th		Ammunition dump at B21.B.0.8. was closed & a new dump with 2/Lt. E. BARKER RFA in charge established at B21.B.2.9. (sheet 28) This dump to be subsequently known as "PINNER" dump.	Phot.
6th		Owing to frequent enemy shelling of locality of earlier	

Army Form C. 2118.

WAR DIARY
or
INTELLIGENCE SUMMARY.
(Erase heading not required.)

Place	Date	Hour	Summary of Events and Information	Remarks and references to Appendices
	10th		E.O.D. Working too of No 1 Section 20th D.A.C. 45 other ranks were presents arrived were distributed b units of 20th Divisional Artillery	Phot. Phot.
	11th 12.00		A quantity of ammunition was brought forward from "PINNER" to BARD dump	Phot. Phot.
	13th		29 other rank reinforcements posted to Brigades and Trench Mortars	
	14th 15th 16th		A quantity of ammunition was brought forward from "PINNER" to BARD dump.	Phot.
	16th		A party was accommodated at group Station A.6.0. to receive surplus rounds for packing and disposal of same.	Phot.
	17th		404 B.V.N ammunition was delivered to Howitzer battery positions.	Phot.
			F.G.C.M. assembled at D.T.C.H.Q. for trial of Gunner T.W. Hughes of Trench Mortars.	Phot.

WAR DIARY
or
INTELLIGENCE SUMMARY

(Erase heading not required.)

Army Form C. 2118.

Place	Date	Hour	Summary of Events and Information	Remarks and references to Appendices
Map of Belgium area France Sheet 28)	7th		H.Q. and "A" Echelon moved back to camps about B.13.B.2.8. (sheet 28). An advanced establishment established about B.1.P.2.1 with 2nd Lieut. E.W. AUSTIN A.P.C. in charge. This dump to be subsequently known as "BARD" dump. To supply of ammunition to 20th D. Artillery. 20 4.5 wagons employed on salvage work from old battery positions for live shell & see kinds of empties.	Phot. Phot.
B.13.B.2.8	8th		100 pack horses & equivalent transport placed at disposal of Brigades.	Phot. Phot.
	8th and 9th		A quantity of ammunition was being brought forward from PINNER to "BARD" dump.	Phot.
	9th		50 other ranks Infantry were attached for work on dumps.	Phot.
	9th		to be retained concentrated by Dump Officers	
	10th		A quantity of ammunition was brought forward from "PINNER" to "BARD" dump. F.G.C.M. assembled at P.A.C., H.Q. for trial of Driver	Phot. Phot.

WAR DIARY
or
INTELLIGENCE SUMMARY

Army Form C. 2118.

Place	Date	Hour	Summary of Events and Information	Remarks and references to Appendices
	19th to 22nd		Ammunition taken forward daily from "PINNER" to "BARD" dump. Extensive salvage work was undertaken with the object of completely clearing old battery position of dumps, shell tracks etc. of live shell & empties.	Phot. Phot.
	22nd		F.G.C.M. assembled for trial of Corporal Marshall A.T. 2nd Mortar.	Phot.
			Ammunition at "BARD" dump was collected & removed to a new dump about B18 B 2.6 (sheet 28) of which E.W. AUSTIN B.F.A. placed in charge. This dump to be subsequently known as "BLETCHLEY" dump.	Phot.
	23rd		F.G.C.M. assembled at D.A.C. HQ for trial of Driver A. Willoughby of A/191st Brigade R.F.A.	Phot.
	23rd to 28th		Ammunition was being lt forward from "PINNER" to "BLETCHLEY" dump. Also extensive salvage work carried out.	Phot.

WAR DIARY or INTELLIGENCE SUMMARY

Army Form C. 2118.

Place	Date	Hour	Summary of Events and Information	Remarks and references to Appendices
	28	9pm	Heavy enemy shelling set fire to "BLETCHLEY" dump, & the dump consisting of about 10,000 rounds ammunition was destroyed with exception of 2000 rounds BX which was saved by Lieut. E.W. AUSTIN, R.F.A., Gunner TATCHELL (No. 3 Section) and Gunner KYLE (Driver, French Mortars). They showed great gallantry & saved the rounds under very trying difficulties, as the boxes were alight, and trying exploding all around them. Disregarding their personal safety they threw buckets of water and wet mud on the boxes and then carried them to a place of safety. In this act of gallantry they were recommended by Col. Hayward 38th Div. for fair immediate reward.	Pho.

WAR DIARY

Army Form C. 2118.

Place	Date	Hour	Summary of Events and Information	Remarks and references to Appendices
B10 B.2.8 (Map of Belgium and France sheet 28)	29th		Salved ammunition at "BEETOLEY" dump was collected & removed to a new position about B17.2.2.9 and a dump established there, to be known as "NUNEATON" dump.	Photo
	29th to 31st		A quantity of ammunition was taken forward from "PINNER" to "NUNEATON" dump, for supply of batteries of 20th Divnl Artillery & 93rd Army Field Artillery Brigade.	Photo

Photo Armytim Nhent RFA
Major for. LT. COLONEL R.F.A.
COMMANDING 20th DIVISIONAL AMMUNITION COLUMN

Aug 16. 1917.

Dear Foster,

On leaving the 20th Division, I want to thank you and all your Column for the support you have always given me.

Please say goodbye to them for me and tell them how grieved I am at having to leave them. I don't think I am at all likely to ever have such another D.A.C. under me.

I am very very sad at having to leave you all especially at this time.

Good-bye

Yours very sincerely,

W. L. Brown.

CONFIDENTIAL

Vol 26

War Diary

of

20th Divisional Ammn. Column.

From: 1.9.17.

To: 30.9.17.

Volume 9.

28031 W3125/M2250 1000m 6/17 M.R.Co.,Ltd. (1367) Forms W3091.   Army Form W. 3091.

Cover for Documents.

Natures of Enclosures.

Notes, or Letters written.

WAR DIARY
or
INTELLIGENCE SUMMARY.
(Erase heading not required.)

Army Form C. 2118.

September

Place	Date	Hour	Summary of Events and Information	Remarks and references to Appendices
Hd. qrs. of Belgian Forces Sheet 28. F.13 F.2.8	1st 2nd		Ammunition was taken forward from PINNER dump to forward dumps BARD (B24.B.6.4) and (B21.B.2.9) to forward dumps BARD (B24.B.6.4) and NUNETON (B19.D.2.3). 22 other rank reinforcements arrived.	WM PM
	3rd 4th		Extensive salvage work (live rounds and empties) carried out in forward area. A quantity of trench collected in EVERDINGHE area (B14.B) and dumped in preparation for work as until wagons lines.	RM
	5th 6th 7th		Ammunition carried daily from PINNER to forward dumps & also extensive salvage work carried out. Trucks collected as wagons were available.	RM
	8th		16 Signaller reinforcements arrived were posted to batteries.	RM

WAR DIARY or INTELLIGENCE SUMMARY

Army Form C. 2118.

September

Place	Date	Hour	Summary of Events and Information	Remarks and references to Appendices
	8th		S.A.A. wagons loaned to R.A. Trench Mortars to assist them in moving forward to camp in evening.	Appx.
	9th		"A" Echelon 20th D.A.C. of "B" Echelon 20th D.A.C. ammunition control of 20th Division "Q" Office for S.A.A. and Howitzer Ammunition taken over from forward dumps.	Appx.
	15th		MIKENGO dump (B24.D9.8) and "BGA" dump (B22.D33) were taken over from 38th Divisional Artillery. "Mikengo" dump placed in charge of an Officer of 76th Brigade Ammunition Column and "BGA" dump in charge of an Officer of 93rd Brigade Ammunition Column.	Appx.

WAR DIARY
or
INTELLIGENCE SUMMARY.

Army Form C. 2118.

September

Place	Date	Hour	Summary of Events and Information	Remarks and references to Appendices
West of Belgium & France Sheet 28 (I 15 B 2.8)	10th		Renewing ammunition on NUNEATON dump was moved to "BIRD" dump, the former being closed. 2 was killed, 1 wounded and 3 horses wounded whilst transporting ammunition from "PINNER" to "BIRD" dump via FERDINGHE - BRIELEN road by enemy bomb.	Apx 5
	11th		21 horses killed by enemy shell fire in No. 2 Section camp.	Apx
	12th 11:45pm		12 other ranks reinforcements sent to Brigades. Several bombs dropped in vicinity of camps.	
	4pm		Heavy enemy shelling in vicinity, tracks, roads, all animals removed from lines.	13th S
	13th 14th 15th		Ammunition lost found by pack animals and dumped in proposed battery positions.	13th K

WAR DIARY
or
INTELLIGENCE SUMMARY.
(Erase heading not required.)

Army Form C. 2118.

September

Place	Date	Hour	Summary of Events and Information	Remarks and references to Appendices
	13th 14th 15th		Ammunition carted forward from "PINNER" to "BARD" and from "BGA" to "MARENGO" for supply of 20th, 29th and 4th Divisional Artilleries, and batteries of 76th & 93rd Field Artillery Brigades. This ammunition included a large quantity of lethal lachrymatory shell.	AJK
	15th		Work on units wagon lines & hutments commenced and camo hurdling material drawn.	RM
	16th		Quantity of ammunition taken up from "PINNER" and "BGA" dumps to forward dumps with assistance of 4th Divisional Ammunition Column.	RJK
	17th		Dumps at "BGA" and MARENGO taken over by 4th Divisional Artillery. Ammunition taken forward from "PINNER" to "BARD" dump. 20 other rank reinforcements arrived, one pukka to brigade.	AJK

WAR DIARY
or
INTELLIGENCE SUMMARY.

(Erase heading not required.)

Army Form C. 2118.

September

Place	Date	Hour	Summary of Events and Information	Remarks and references to Appendices
	18th		69 other ranks reinforcements arrived were posted to Brigades. Trench Mortars and D.A.C.	AJMS
	18th 19th		Large quantities of ammunition including lethal & lachrymatory shells were taken to special battery positions by pack animals.	AJ&T
	20th 21st 22nd 23rd		Quantities of bricks (from ruined houses in ELVERDINGHE) also of galvanized iron, timber, tarred felting, and concrete slabs drawn from R.E. dumps	AJMR
	23rd 24th		11 other rank reinforcements rcd. to Brigades. Work on huts, nets & stables pushed on rapidly, a number of natives of B.W.I.R. being withdrawn from ammunition dumps to assist in the labour.	AJMS
	25th 26th		Large quantities of material taken forward dumped in selected positions under cover of darkness, for construction of new gun positions	AJMS
	27th 28th		"B" Echelon, 20th D.A.C. under instructions from	AJMS
	29th			AJMS

WAR DIARY
or
INTELLIGENCE SUMMARY.
(Erase heading not required.)

Army Form C. 2118.

September

Place	Date	Hour	Summary of Events and Information	Remarks and references to Appendices
Map of Belgium & France Sheet 28 (J 13 & J.19)	29th 30th		20th Division "D" moved back to reserve area. Assistance given to battery wagon lines to take ammunition to battery positions. Large quantity of ammunition delivered to special positions, by pack animals.	R.S.t
	30th			
	NOTE:		Ammunition taken forward on 20th and previous to that date was for use in the operations carried out N.E. of LANGEMARCK on 20th September 1917.	F.S.t

M Fisher
LT. COLONEL R.F.A.
COMMANDING 20th DIVISIONAL AMMUNITION COLUMN

CONFIDENTIAL

M 27

WAR DIARY
of
20th. Divnl. Ammn. Column.

From 1st October to 31st October 1917.

VOL. 10.

Army Form C. 2118.

WAR DIARY
or
INTELLIGENCE SUMMARY.
(Erase heading not required.)

October 1917.

Instructions regarding War Diaries and Intelligence Summaries are contained in F. S. Regs., Part II. and the Staff Manual respectively. Title pages will be prepared in manuscript.

Place	Date	Hour	Summary of Events and Information	Remarks and references to Appendices
	1st.		Quantity of constructional material drawn from R.E. dump dumped in No.1 Sections camp. Ammunition taken forward from PINNER dump (B24D2P) to BARD dump (B34B64).	A.M.
	2nd		75 pack animals removed ammunition from HANLEY Deauville Station ( ) to battery positions. Ammunition taken forward from PINNER to BARD dump	P.M.
	3rd		Quantity of constructional material stored in No.1 Section camp taken forward dumped at SANDY HOUSE B18c12½. Ammunition taken forward from PINNER to BARD dump	P.M.
	4th		General salvage work carried out in forward area. Constructional material taken forward returned for 91st Brigade R.F.A.	A.M.

Army Form C. 2118.

WAR DIARY
or
INTELLIGENCE SUMMARY.

(Erase heading not required.)

October 1917

Instructions regarding War Diaries and Intelligence Summaries are contained in F. S. Regs., Part II. and the Staff Manual respectively. Title pages will be prepared in manuscript.

Place	Date	Hour	Summary of Events and Information	Remarks and references to Appendices
	5th		Salvage work carried out in forward area. Ammunition carted forward from PINNER & BARD dumps	PWK
	6th		11 Remounts drawn from PROVEN railhead (?) Ammunition drawn from Guards Dump at TURQUE FARM was taken forward & dumped for 91st Brigade RFA. Constructional material dumps from RE dump and stored in No.1 Sections camp.	PWK
	7th		Lieut E W AUSTIN and party at BARD and Lieut E. BARKER and party at PINNER dumps were relieved by parties of 19th Divisional Artillery.	PWK
	8th		Ammunition drawn from TURQUE FARM dumps (BISA 9.9). Taken forward & dumped for 91st Brigade RFA, also constructional material	PWK

WAR DIARY or INTELLIGENCE SUMMARY

Army Form C. 2118.

October 1917

Place	Date	Hour	Summary of Events and Information	Remarks and references to Appendices
	9th		Ammunition delivered by pack animals to batteries of 9th Bde. A.F.A.	Apx.
	10th		58 other ranks reinforcements arrived were posted to Brigades.	Apx 5
			Party of 15 other ranks detailed for work on ammunition train & placed under orders of O.C. Corps Ammunition Park	
	11th 12th		Ammunition drawn from TORQUE FARM dump and delivered to batteries of 9th Bde. A.F.A.	Apx.
	10th		45 other rank reinforcements arrived were posted to Brigades and D.A.C.	
			Ammunition was salved from an old battery position at C.7.c.5.7. taken to Deauville Siding at B.16.A.7.8.	Apx.

WAR DIARY or INTELLIGENCE SUMMARY

Army Form C. 2118.

October 1917

Place	Date	Hour	Summary of Events and Information	Remarks and references to Appendices
	14th		10 G.S. wagons detailed to collect kit etc. of any Officers and men of 91st Brigade out of action for the time being.	89M2
	15th		10 G.S. wagons of forage drawn from RE dump and delivered to 91st Brigade dump at U.27.B.4.8½. Ammunition drawn from TORQUE FARM dump & delivered D/92 battery position.	89M
	16th and		10 G.S. wagons of forage drawn from RE dump delivered to U.27.A.6.8, also 10 G.S. wagons forage to U.27.B.4.8½.	89M
	17th		Ammunition drawn from TORQUE FARM dump and delivered to battery positions.	89M
	18th		Advance party of 1 Officer, 3 N.C.O.s proceeded to SOMEL-LE-GRAND (Sheet 57E) W.13.c) to take over billets.	89M

WAR DIARY
or
INTELLIGENCE SUMMARY.

(Erase heading not required.)

October 1917

Army Form C. 2118.

Place	Date	Hour	Summary of Events and Information	Remarks and references to Appendices
Belgium & France Sheet 28 I.13.2.8	19th		Echelons & Sections were filled up to establishment. Packing of wagons & limbers commenced in preparation for expected move. Camps were cleaned up and inventories prepared of all stores & equipment to be handed over.	AMR
	20th		Advance party of 350th D.A.C. took over H.Q. and Section camps.	AMS
	21st	20AM / 21AM	The Column entrained at regular times & had returned to H.Q. & No.1 Section at PROVEN railhead. No.2 Section at PESELHOEK railhead.	AMR
	22nd		The Column detrained at regular intervals at PERONNE (I.28.d.5.0) Sheet 62c and marched to temporary camps in NURLU (D.4 central) Sheet 62c	AMR

Army Form C. 2118.

WAR DIARY
or
INTELLIGENCE SUMMARY.
(Erase heading not required.)

October 1917

Instructions regarding War Diaries and Intelligence Summaries are contained in F. S. Regs., Part II. and the Staff Manual respectively. Title pages will be prepared in manuscript.

Place	Date	Hour	Summary of Events and Information	Remarks and references to Appendices
	23rd 24th		Pending relief of 40th Divisional Ammunition Column reoccupation of their camps in vicinity. Horse lines improved, vehicles and equipment overhauled, refitments where necessary.	Pas. Pas.
	25th 26th 27th		Various fatigues performed for Infantry, Engineers & Trench Mortars. Practically all 98 wagons of each Echelon employed.	Pas.
	28th		H.Q. and Sections moved into camps vacated by 40th D.A.C.	Pas.
	30th		Lieut. E.W. AUSTIN M.C. taken in charge of dump ... from 40th D.A.C. strength about W. & E. (Shels &c.)	Pas.
	29th 30th 31st		Numerous G.S. wagon fatigues carried out.	Pas.

R.H. Denman Capt. for Lt. Colonel R.F.A.
COMMANDING 20th DIVISIONAL AMMUNITION COLUMN

CONFIDENTIAL.

WAR DIARY

OF

20th Divisional Ammunition Column A.I.F.

From 1st Nov. to 30th November 1917.

VOL: 11.

WAR DIARY

20th Divisional Ammn Column
November 1917.

Army Form C. 2118.

INTELLIGENCE SUMMARY.

Place	Date	Hour	Summary of Events and Information	Remarks and references to Appendices
NURLU (Sheet 62c - D14 A and B)	1st to 13th	(Various)	A number of G.S. wagons detailed daily for all Divisional fatigues, for R.E's, Infantry & Trench Mortars.	P.145.
	14th		Ammunition unloading parties detailed to proceed to WOOLWICH dump (Sheet 57c W2B) for unloading of Decauville train, reloading of G.S. wagons to proceed to forward area, there to dump ammunition under orders of Officer of 92nd Brigade RFA.	P.146.
	14th		F.G.C.M. assembled at Court Martial Hut at SOREL (Sheet 57c W13c) for trial of 12595 Driver O. Mullows, No. 2 Section	P.147.
	15th 16th 17th		Various G.S. wagon fatigues, mural ammunition working parties detailed. Wagons loaned to Brigades to assist them to move	P.148.

WAR DIARY
or
INTELLIGENCE SUMMARY.
(Erase heading not required.)

Army Form C. 2118.

November 1917.

Place	Date	Hour	Summary of Events and Information	Remarks and references to Appendices
N.V.R.L.V	17th		No. 1 Section vacated their camp for 20th Divnl. Train M.S.C. otherwise joined up with Nos. 2 and 3 Sections.	Appx
Sheet 62c D.14.A+B	18th		G.S. wagon fatigues, and 3600 A and 3600 AX drawn from Corps Ammunition Park Scainville riding Section camps for refilling of Brigade refilled in Section camps for refilling of D.A.C.	Appx H S
	19th 20th		G.S. wagon fatigues, ammunition working parties detailed.	Appx
	21st		H.Q. and Nos. 1 and 2 Sections moved forward to wagon lines about W.13.B (Sheet 57c) near SOREL. No. 3 Section moved forward to wagon lines as above.	Appx H+S
W.13.B Sheet 57c	22nd		Forward ammunition dump established in old battery position about R.25.D.5.6 (Sheet 57c) and Lieut. H. MAYNARD was placed in charge.	Appx N

Army Form C. 2118.

WAR DIARY
or
INTELLIGENCE SUMMARY.
(Erase heading not required.)

November 1917.

Place	Date	Hour	Summary of Events and Information	Remarks and references to Appendices
E.13.B (Sheet 57c)	22nd		Teams & limbers detailed to bring in 2 captured guns (German) from about LE QUENNET FARM (M.7.A.6.0) map of GOUZEAUCOURT.	Appx.
	23rd 24th 25th 26th		G.S. wagon fatigues carried out. Salvage of all natures of ammunition carried out along roads & tracks in forward area, such ammunition being taken to forward dumps at R.25.D.5.6.	Appx.
NURLU	27th		H.Q. & Sections moved back to old camps in NURLU owing to shortage of water in forward area.	Appx.
	28th and 29th		G.S. wagon fatigues including the withdrawal of all smoke shell from forward dump R.25.D.5.6. and delivery of same to Corps Reserve at Decauville railway siding in square D.9.B. (Sheet 62C).	Appx. Appx.
	30th		G.S. wagon fatigues carried out.	Appx.

R.W. Bennenn Capt R.A. for
LT. COLONEL R.F.A.
COMMANDING 20TH DIVISIONAL AMMUNITION

CONFIDENTIAL.

WAR DIARY.
OF
20th Divisional Ammunition Column B.E.F.

From 1st Dec. to 31st December 1917.

VOL: 12

Vol 29

Army Form C. 2118.

WAR DIARY
or
INTELLIGENCE SUMMARY.
(Erase heading not required.)

December 1917

Instructions regarding War Diaries and Intelligence Summaries are contained in F. S. Regs., Part II. and the Staff Manual respectively. Title pages will be prepared in manuscript.

Place	Date	Hour	Summary of Events and Information	Remarks and references to Appendices
N.U.R.L.S. (Sheet 57c)	1st		Pack animals with ammunition sent to 91st Brigade R.F.A. also 30 R.A. wagons loaded at dump sent to 91st and 256th Brigades R.F.A.	J.U.R.
	2nd		Ammunition dump at Q.25 central taken over from 6th D.A. and Lieut E.W. AUSTIN placed in charge. Ammunition drawn from WOOLWICH ammunition dump delivered to 91st and 256th Brigades.	J.M.R
	3rd		30 pack animals, saddlery & drivers loaned to 61st Division for work.	J.U.R.
	4th		Ammunition drawn from dump at Q.25 central and dumped in 256th and 436th Battery wagon lines. Pack animals and 48 R.A. wagons of ammunition sent to 91st Brigade.	J.U.R.
	5th		61 reinforcements animals were distributed to Brigades and D.A.C.	J.U.R.

WAR DIARY
INTELLIGENCE SUMMARY

Army Form C. 2118.

December 1917

Place	Date	Hour	Summary of Events and Information	Remarks and references to Appendices
NURLU (Sheet 57c)	6th		18 RA wagons ammunition taken from dump Q.25 central to 91st & 236th Brigades.	9 MB
	7th		G.S. wagon fatigues, 9 RA wagons ammunition delivered to 463rd B.	9 MB
	8th		Woolwich ammunition dump closed.	9 MB
	9th		36 reinforcements other ranks distributed to Brigades.	9 MB R & S
	9th 10th		G.S. wagon fatigues ammunition delivered to 91st Brigade APA	9 MB
	11th		91st Brigade field gun tip to be established all preparations made for expected move.	9 MB
	12th 13th			
	14th		H.Q. Nos. 2 and 3 Sections moved off from NURLU and travelling via PERONNE occupied billets in vicinity of DERNANCOURT (Map of ALBERT) No. 1 Section remained behind with rear [party?] of 91st Brigade RFA.	9 MB

Army Form C. 2118.

WAR DIARY
or
INTELLIGENCE SUMMARY.
(Erase heading not required.)

December 1917

Place	Date	Hour	Summary of Events and Information	Remarks and references to Appendices
MARCH	15th		H.Q. Nos 2 and 3 Sections left DERNANCOURT and marched to billets in ACHEUX and LOUVENCOURT via ALBERT. (refer map LENS 11)	Appx
	16th		H.Q. Nos 2 and 3 Sections left ACHEUX and LOUVENCOURT and marched to billets in TOUTENCOURT. (map LENS 11).	Appx
	17th		H.Q. Nos 2 and 3 Sections left AMPLIER and marched to billets in GRAND and PETIT BOUVET and PREVENT with DAC. HQ in PREVENT.	Appx
LINE OF MARCH	21st		Resting in PREVENT (map LENS 11).	Appx
	22nd		No.1 Section arrived billetted in NUNCQ and PREVENT.	Appx
	22nd		H.Q. and Sections left PREVENT area marched to billets in TROISVAUX, CONTEVILLE and BELVAL north of ST POL. (map LENS 11).	Appx
	23rd		H.Q. No. 1 Section left TROISVAUX to march to billets in RODECQ. (map HAZEBROUCK 5A).	Appx
	24th			Appx

WAR DIARY
or
INTELLIGENCE SUMMARY.

Army Form C. 2118.

December 1917.

Place	Date	Hour	Summary of Events and Information	Remarks and references to Appendices
	25th to 29th		Resting in ROBECQ area.	
	30th		HQ and all Sections marched from ROBECQ area and occupied billets in vicinity of CROIX ROUGE north of STRAZEELE (Map of Hazebrouck 5A).	
	31st		HQ and all Sections marched from CROIX ROUGE and occupied rest camps at CROIX de POPERINGHE in Square M.32.b. (Map of Belgium & France Sheet 28)	

R. Denman
Lt. Col. R.A.
for LT. COLONEL R.T.
COMMANDING 20th DIVISIONAL AMMUNITION COLUMN.

CONFIDENTIAL.

WAR DIARY.

OF

20th Divisional Ammunition Column.

From 1st Jany to 31st Jany 1918.

VOL. 1

WAR DIARY
or
INTELLIGENCE SUMMARY.
(Erase heading not required.)

Army Form C. 2118.

January 1918.

Place	Date	Hour	Summary of Events and Information	Remarks and references to Appendices
CROIX de POPERINGHE Square M32B Sheet 28	14th to 20th inclusive		HQ and Sections remained in rest area, carried out repair and improvements on existing camps, latrines, stables & harness rooms. Also a proportion of IX th Corps daily G.S. wagon fatigues were carried out including thaw precaution detail on several occasions.	
ZEVECOTEN Square G35c Sheet 28	21st		HQ. and Sections marched out, occupied camps about ZEVECOTEN (Square G35c Sheet 28) in relief of 37th Divisional Ammunition Column who marched back to CROIX de POPERINGHE camps	
	22nd to		G.S. wagon fatigues were carried out daily under orders received from A.D. of S. and T. IXth Corps. In accordance with Fourth Army orders, material was	
	30th		indented for and protective earth and bag walls erected round all latrines stables as a precaution against hostile bombing	

Army Form C. 2118.

WAR DIARY
or
INTELLIGENCE SUMMARY.
(Erase heading not required.)

January 1918.

Place	Date	Hour	Summary of Events and Information	Remarks and references to Appendices
LEUZE COTEN. Square G.9.c. Sheet 28.	30th		The Column as a unit of 20th Division was transferred from IXth to XXIInd Corps, but remained in same camps.	Appx I
	30th and 31st		G.S. wagon fatigues & camp improvements continued.	Appx

F.H. Renman Capt & Adjt
LT. COLONEL
COMMANDING 20th DIVISIONAL AMMUNITION COLUMN

CONFIDENTIAL.

WA 31

WAR DIARY.

OF

20th D.A.C.

From 1st to 28th February 1918.

(6339) Wt. W160/M3016 1,500,000 10/17 McA & W Ltd (E 1898) Forms W3091.   Army Form W.3091.

Cover for Documents.

Nature of Enclosures.

Notes, or Letters written.

WAR DIARY
or
INTELLIGENCE SUMMARY.
(Erase heading not required.)

Army Form C. 2118.

February 1918.

Place: West of Belgium & France (9.35c) Sheet 28

Date	Hour	Summary of Events and Information	Remarks and references to Appendices
1st to 6th		Various G.S. wagon fatigues carried out under orders of A.D. of S. and T. XXII Corps.	
6th		No. 3 Section marched out & occupied camp near HALLEBAST (M32D Sheet 28 map of Belgium & France).	
7th to 16th		Various G.S. wagon fatigues carried out under orders of A.D. of S. and T. XXII Corps.	
16th		Ammunition dumps and Salvage parties were relieved by parties of 37th Divisional Ammunition Column. 2 Officers and 4 N.C.Os proceeded to ROUEN to enlarge course in language, manners and customs of Indian personnel expected to join the Column.	
17th		20th D.A.C. were relieved by 37th D.A.C. marching out; occupied camps about CROIX DE POPERINGHE (M32D Sheet 28).	
18th		Vehicles equipment overhauled, necessary remedy repairs effected etc.	

WAR DIARY
or
INTELLIGENCE SUMMARY
(Erase heading not required.)

Army Form C. 2118.

February 1918.

Place	Date	Hour	Summary of Events and Information	Remarks and references to Appendices
Line of March	19th		H.Q. and Sections marched out from CROIX DE POPERINGHE & billetted in MORBECQUE area (map HAZEBROUCK 5A). 27 other rank reinforcements arrived from Base Depot.	JB
	20th to 22nd		Resting at MORBECQUE area.	JB
	23rd		At regular periods H.Q. and Sections entrained at STEENBECQUE (map HAZEBROUCK 5A)	JB
	24th		Upon arrival H.Q. and Sections detrained at NESLE (I.19.A Sheet 66.D) H.Q., Nos 2 and 3 Sections marched to and occupied billets in ROUY-LE-PETIT (I.10 central Sheet 66.D). No. 3 Section marched to & occupied billets in OFFOY (J.15.C Sheet 66.D).	JB
	25th to 28th		Resting in ROUY-LE-PETIT and OFFOY, a few G.S. wagon fatigues carried out, and also various repairs to vehicles etc., and renewals of equipment, stores.	JB

Edward Barker
Lt. Colonel
Commanding 20th Divisional Ammunition Column.

20th Divisional Artillery.

20th DIVISIONAL AMMUNITION COLUMN R.F.A.

MARCH 1918

YA 32

CONFIDENTIAL.

WAR DIARY
of
20th Divl. Ammunition Column.

From 1st to 31st March 1918

Vol III

(6339) Wt. W160/M3016 1,500,000 10/17 McA & W Ltd. (E 1898) Forms W3091.   Army Form W.3091.

Cover for Documents.

Nature of Enclosures.

Notes, or Letters written.

Army Form C. 2118.

WAR DIARY
or
INTELLIGENCE SUMMARY. March 1918.
(Erase heading not required.)

Place	Date	Hour	Summary of Events and Information	Remarks and references to Appendices
	1st to 20th		H.Q. and Sections resting at ROUY-LE-PETIT and OFFOY (I.10.B and D and J.15.C. Sheet 66D) respectively.	
	21st		No.1 Section joined 91st Brigade R.F.A. and with that Brigade moved forward occupied camp about SAINT SIMON (L.34.A Sheet 66D).	
			No.2 Section joined 92nd Brigade R.F.A. and with that Brigade moved forward occupied camp about AUBIGNY (K.11.D Sheet 66D).	
			No.3 Section under orders of "Q" Office 20th Division moved forward occupied camp about VILLERS-ST.-CHRISTOPHE (K.9.D Sheet 66D).	
			All these moves were carried out in accordance with the terms of the XVIIIth Corps Defence Scheme	

Army Form C. 2118.

WAR DIARY
or
INTELLIGENCE SUMMARY.
(Erase heading not required.)

March 1918.

Place	Date	Hour	Summary of Events and Information	Remarks and references to Appendices
	22nd		Subsequent to this date 21st March 1918 Headquarters 20th D.A.C. was not in touch with Sections and moved independently according to following details. Headquarters marched from ROUY-LE-PETIT intending to occupy camp vacated by No. 1 Section, but after passing through VOYENNES (J7c Sheet 66D) turned back to ROUY-LE-PETIT as enemy was reported to be advancing.	
	23rd		Headquarters left ROUY-LE-PETIT and marched via NESLE, CURCHY and GRUNY to GOYENCOURT (M.1.D Sheet 66D) and camped for the night.	
	24th		Remained at GOYENCOURT.	

Army Form C. 2118.

WAR DIARY
or
INTELLIGENCE SUMMARY.
(Erase heading not required.)

March 1918.

Place	Date	Hour	Summary of Events and Information	Remarks and references to Appendices
	25th		Headquarters left GOYENCOURT marched via ANDECHY to ERCHE'S and camped for night.	
	26th		Headquarters left ERCHES and marched via ARVILLERS and PLESSIER to MOREUIL, and billetted for night.	
	27th		Headquarters left MOREUIL and marched via AILLY-SUR-NOYE to JUMEL and billetted for night.	
West of AMIENS	28th		Headquarters left JUMEL and marched via ORESMAUX and ST SAUFLIEU to NEUVILLE-SOUS-LOEUILLY and billetted for night.	
West of March AMIENS	29th 30th 31st		Headquarters remained at NEUVILLE-SOUS-LOEUILLY.	

M. Mohn L. Col.

Vol 33

War Diary
of
20th Divnl. Amm. Col.

1-4-18 to 30-4-18.

Vol: 4.

Confidential.

Army Form C. 2118.

WAR DIARY
or
INTELLIGENCE SUMMARY.
(Erase heading not required.)

April 1918.

Instructions regarding War Diaries and Intelligence Summaries are contained in F. S. Regs., Part II. and the Staff Manual respectively. Title pages will be prepared in manuscript.

Place	Date	Hour	Summary of Events and Information	Remarks and references to Appendices
	5th		Headquarters remained at NEUVILLE-SOUS-LOEUILLY (Map of Amiens) awaiting orders.	
	6th			
	7th		Left NEUVILLE marched via POIX and HORNOY into billets at SENARPONT. (Map of Dieppe.)	
	8th		Nos 1 and 2 Sections arrived in SENARPONT and occupied billets near that town.	
	9th		No. 1 Section left SENARPONT and marched to THELLULOYE - L'ABBAYE. Headquarters and No. 2 Sections remained at SENARPONT awaiting orders.	
	10th		No. 1 Section left THELLULOYE - L'ABBAYE and marched overland via (from III Corps) from Town Major of that town obtaining orders. Headquarters and No. 2 Section remained at SENARPONT.	
	11th		Headquarters and No. 2 Section left SENARPONT marched to billeted in Faubourg LES PLANCHES (south of ABBEVILLE)	
	12th & 13th		Headquarters No. 2 Section remained at LES PLANCHES, refitting.	

WAR DIARY
or
INTELLIGENCE SUMMARY.

April 1918.

Army Form C. 2118.

Place	Date	Hour	Summary of Events and Information	Remarks and references to Appendices
	16th		No. 2 Section left LES PLANCHES & marched to LAMOTTE-BREBIERE. (Square N15D Sheet 62.D.), receiving orders from 5th Australian Division at the latter place.	78
	17th		Headquarters remained at LES PLANCHES.	
	18th		Headquarters left LES PLANCHES marching as far as BETTENCOURT, billeted for the night.	
	19th		Headquarters left BETTENCOURT marching via PICQUIGNY, AILLY-SUR-SOMME and south of AMIENS arrived at GUISY (Part of AMIENS). After ascertaining that there was no available accommodation in GUISY, Headquarters moved back to RIVERY (North-East of AMIENS) & occupied billets in that place.	
	20th		Headquarters 20th D.A.C. office was established in LAMOTTE-BREBIERE but all transport remained at wagon line in RIVERY.	

WAR DIARY
or
INTELLIGENCE SUMMARY.

Army Form C. 2118.

April 1918

Place	Date	Hour	Summary of Events and Information	Remarks and references to Appendices
	20th		D.A.C. became responsible for ammunition supply of 91st and 92nd Brigades & took over ammunition dump at N.21.c.5.2. Lieut. A.T. GULLIVER, M.C. being placed in charge. Ammunition received at the dump from Corps Ammunition Park was issued & delivered to batteries of 91st, 92nd and 79.	B.
	22nd		91st Brigade's A.F.A.	
	23rd		Ammunition issued & delivered to 91st, 92nd, 179th and 75. 91st Brigade's R.F.A.	
	24th		Owing to operations pending & heavy enemy shelling of that area No 1 and 2 Sections moved back & established camps N.E. of CAMON in Square M.11.A Sheet 62.D. A temporary ammunition dump was also formed in this locality, & ammunition supplied to batteries, but later the old dump at N.21.c.5.2. was re-established	B.

Army Form C. 2118.

WAR DIARY
or
INTELLIGENCE SUMMARY.

(Erase heading not required.)

April 1918.

Instructions regarding War Diaries and Intelligence Summaries are contained in F. S. Regs., Part II. and the Staff Manual respectively. Title pages will be prepared in manuscript.

Place	Date	Hour	Summary of Events and Information	Remarks and references to Appendices
	25th & 26th		Assistance rendered to batteries in ammunition supply	A/
	26th		No. 2 Section moved forward reoccupied camp about Square N9D Sheet 62D	A/
	27th		Assisted Trench Mortar batteries to take up ammunition material	A/
	28th		Headquarters No. 1 and 2 Sections moved back billeted in vicinity of SALOUEL (South West of AMIENS) Resting at SALOUEL opportunity was taken to effect necessary repairs replace deficiencies in equipment etc.	A/ A/
	29th		Headquarters and Nos. 1 and 2 Sections left SALOUEL and marched West of Amiens, thence via ST JUST, VIGNACOURT and POMART to billeted in BERNEUIL (South of BERNAVILLE West of LENS.	A/ A/
	30th			

Army Form C. 2118.

WAR DIARY
or
INTELLIGENCE SUMMARY.
(Erase heading not required.)

April 1918.

Instructions regarding War Diaries and Intelligence Summaries are contained in F. S. Regs., Part II. and the Staff Manual respectively. Title pages will be prepared in manuscript.

Place	Date	Hour	Summary of Events and Information	Remarks and references to Appendices
			The last march (commencing April 28th) was consequent upon the transfer of the 28th Divisional Artillery from Fourth to First Army. During the whole month No. 3, or the S.A.A. Section, was detached from the Column, and the order of Q.B. the 20th D. vision.	

W Rabin Robert
Lieutenant Bombardier

3' Section DAC

Army Form C. 2118.

WAR DIARY
or
INTELLIGENCE SUMMARY.
(Erase heading not required.)

Place	Date	Hour	Summary of Events and Information	Remarks and references to Appendices
ROUY LE PETIT	21.3.18	5.0pm	Ordered into action. Marched to VILLERS ST CHRISTOPHE where remained all night. Issued ammunition.	AW.05 AW.05
VILLERS ST CHRISTOPHE	22.3.18	3.0pm	Withdrew to SANCOURT-TOULIS. Issued 300 boxes S.A.A. from VILLERS ST CHRISTOPHE.	AW.05
	23.3.18	12 M.N.	Withdrew to OFFOY-VOYENNES. Withdrew to LANGUEVOISIN. 4.0pm withdrew to BILLANCOURT. Ordered to move to RETHONVILLERS. Refilled ammunition from CARRÉPUIS. Issued ammunition	AW.05
RETHONVILLERS	24.3.18	3.30pm	Withdrew to SEPT-FOURS - CREMERY when enemy bombed.	AW.05
CREMERY	25.3.18	1.0am	Withdrew to FRESNOY-LES-ROYE and refilled from CARRÉPUIS. 11.30am withdrew to GOYENCOURT. 4.0pm withdrew to LE QUESNIL	AW.05
LE QUESNIL	26.3.18	4.30pm	Arrived LE QUESNIL. 1.0pm ordered to withdraw to MEZIÈRES - VILLERS-aux-ERABLES. Issued 3 wagon loads at Rubira.	AW.05
VILLERS-aux-ERABLES	27.3.18		Issuing Ammunition and rations	AW.05
" "	28.3.18	10.0am	Withdrew to cross roads between DEMUIN - MOREUIL - MOREUIL remained until 2.0pm withdrew to DOMMART. 12.0v.s. withdrew to SAINS-en-AMIENOIS	AW.05
SAINS-en-AMIENOIS	29.3.18		Issuing ammunition and conveying to Infantry under instructions from "Q" Refilled by Motor Lorries	AW.05
" "	30.3.18		Issuing ammunition. Refilled by Motor Lorries	AW.05
" "	31.3.18		Issuing ammunition. Refilled by Motor Lorries	AW.05
" "	1.4.18		Issuing ammunition. 10.0pm withdrew to QUEVAUVILLERS	AW.05
QUEVAUVILLERS	2.4.18	6.0am	Arrived QUEVAUVILLERS. Reported action	AW.05
	3.4.18	11.0am	Shifted to NAMPS-au-MONTS	AW.05

Army Form C. 2118.

WAR DIARY
or
INTELLIGENCE SUMMARY.

(Erase heading not required.)

Instructions regarding War Diaries and Intelligence
Summaries are contained in F. S. Regs., Part II.
and the Staff Manual respectively. Title pages
will be prepared in manuscript.

Place	Date	Hour	Summary of Events and Information	Remarks and references to Appendices
NAMPS-AU-MONT	4-4-18		At NAMPS-AU-MONT Awaiting Orders	
"	5-4-18		– do –	
"	6-4-18	2.0pm	Moved to QUEVAUVILLERS	
QUEVAUVILLERS	7-4-18		Awaiting Orders	
"	8-4-18		"	
"	9-4-18	9.0am	Moved to BROCOURT-LIOMER All ranks in open again	
BROCOURT	10-4-18	10.0am	Moved to HUPPY Men in billets for first time since 21-3-18	
BRECOURT-MESNIL	11-4-18	11.0am	Moved to GREAAUL-MESNIL All ranks in billets	
LONGROY	12-4-18		Moved to LONGROY Checked and drew ammunition up to Establishment	
"	13-4-18		Awaiting Orders	
"	14-4-18		– " –	
"	15-4-18		– " –	
"	16-4-18	7.0pm	Moved to EAUCOURT	
EAUCOURT	18-4-18	10am	Arrived EAUCOURT 11.0am moved to VILLERS-L'HOPITAL	
VILLERS L'HOPITAL	19-4-18	9.4am	Moved to HERLIN-LE-SEC Enemy bombing village	
HERLIN-LE-SEC	20-4-18	9.0am	Moved to MINGOVAL Issued ammunition	
MINGOVAL	21-4-18		Refitting Personnel Animals & Vehicles	
"	22-4-18		Awaiting Orders	
"	23-4-18		"	
"	24-4-18		"	

Army Form C. 2118.

WAR DIARY
or
INTELLIGENCE SUMMARY.
(Erase heading not required.)

Instructions regarding War Diaries and Intelligence
Summaries are contained in F. S. Regs., Part II.
and the Staff Manual respectively. Title pages
will be prepared in manuscript.

Place	Date	Hour	Summary of Events and Information	Remarks and references to Appendices
MINGOVAL	25-4-18		Awaiting Orders	aw25
"	26-4-18		"	aw26
"	27-4-18		"	aw27
"	28-4-18		"	aw28
"	29-4-18		"	aw29
"	30-4-18		"	aw30
"	1-5-18		"	aw1
"	2-5-18		"	aw2
"	3-5-18	2 pm	Marched to ABLAIN ST NAZAIRE	aw3
ABLAIN ST NAZAIRE	4-5-18		Under orders from D.A.C. H.Q.	aw4
"	5-5-18			aw5

Total Rounds S.A.A. received 21-3-18 - 5-5-18 4,500,000 rds
Total Grenades received   3,600

A. M. W. Bowel. Capt RCA
Comdg No 3 Section 20th D.A.C.

No. 8 SECTION,
20th DIVISIONAL
AMMUNITION COLUMN,
R.F.A.
No. —
Date 9.5.18

Dear Foster

Your No 1 Section will have joined you ere this & I wish to say that whilst it was with me everything required of it was done in a highly satisfactory manner. I have known Hamilton some time - he is very proud of his Section & it certainly does him credit.

We have been very near each other several times but up to now have not had the pleasure of running up against you - but hope to in the near future.

My very best wishes
Yours Sincerely
H L Riley

6.4.18.

WR 34

WAR DIARY

of

20th Divl. Amm. Column.

from 1st to 31st May 1918

Vol V.

Confidential

(6339) Wt. W160/M3016 1,500,000 10/17 McA & W Ltd (E1898) Forms W3091.   Army Form W.3091.

Cover for Documents.

Nature of Enclosures.

Notes, or Letters written.

WAR DIARY
or
INTELLIGENCE SUMMARY.

Army Form C. 2118.

May 1918

Place	Date	Hour	Summary of Events and Information	Remarks and references to Appendices
Issu & March Maly LENS II	1st		Headquarters, Nos 1 and 2 Sections left BERNEUIL & marched to & billeted in BEAUCOURT.	
	2nd		Headquarters, Nos 1 and 2 Sections left BEAUCOURT marching via FREVENT arrived at HOUVIN-HOUVIGNEUL & billeted.	
	3rd		Resting in HOUVIN-HOUVIGNEUL & awaiting orders.	
	4th		Headquarters, Nos 1 and 2 Sections left HOUVIN-HOUVIGNEUL marching via TINQUES arrived at GOUY-SERVINS relieving No 3 (Canadian Divl. Auxto Colun) reoccupying camps of 3rd (Canadian Divl. Auxto Colun) at that place. Lieut. E.T. WILSON and party detailed to take over PANET dump (near ABLAIN ST-NAZAIRE) ammunition supply on the Decauville Light Railway system. No. 3 Section situate in camp at ABLAIN ST-NAZAIRE (Square X 10 A and B, Sheet 36B) came under orders of O.C. 20th D.A.C.	
GOUY-SERVINS Q 35 A Map Sheet 36 B	5th			

Army Form C. 2118.

WAR DIARY
or
INTELLIGENCE SUMMARY.
(Erase heading not required.)

May 1918

Instructions regarding War Diaries and Intelligence Summaries are contained in F. S. Regs., Part II and the Staff Manual respectively. Title pages will be prepared in manuscript.

Place	Date	Hour	Summary of Events and Information	Remarks and references to Appendices
GOUY – SERVINS Square Q.35.D Sheet 36B	5th 6th 7th		R.E. material obtained for repair of & improvements to camps. Sunday repairs to vehicles equipment effected in No. 2 Section placed at disposal of 9nd Brigade	
	8th		with that Brigade came under orders of 24th Divl. Artillery. No. 2 Section proceeded to AIX-NOULETTE (R.22.D Sheet 36.B) and supplied ammunition. 92nd Brigade, refilling from the echelon of No.1 Section. The late Section refilled at PANET dump.	
	9th 10th 11th 12th		57 reinforcements arrived were posted to Brigades. Trench Mortars, and D.A.C. No. 2 Section supplied batteries of 92nd Brigade with ammunition. Nos. 1 and 3 Sections carried out various G.S. wagon fatigues.	

Army Form C. 2118.

WAR DIARY
or
INTELLIGENCE SUMMARY.
(Erase heading not required.)

May 1918.

Instructions regarding War Diaries and Intelligence Summaries are contained in F. S. Regs., Part II. and the Staff Manual respectively. Title pages will be prepared in manuscript.

Place	Date	Hour	Summary of Events and Information	Remarks and references to Appendices
Gouy-Servins Square Q35d Sheet 36B	13th		No. 2 Section returned from AIX-NOULETTE to their original camp at GOUY-SERVINS.	JH
	14th 15th 16th		All Sections engaged upon various G.S. wagon fatigues. 35 reinforcements arrived were posted to Brigades, Trench Mortars & D.A.C.	JH
			36 recruits were drawn & distributed between Brigades & Sections & D.A.C.	JH
	17th 18th 19th		All Sections engaged upon various G.S. wagon fatigues and camp repairs & improvements etc.	JH
	20th 21st 22nd		No. 1 and 2 Sections drew ammunition from PAWET dump & filled to an establishment of 100 rounds per gun at howitzer, the selected (unoccupied) rear positions of Batteries of 9th and 9th Army Brigades in accordance with 20th Divisional Artillery Defence Scheme.	JH

Army Form C. 2118.

WAR DIARY
or
INTELLIGENCE SUMMARY.
(Erase heading not required.)

May 1918.

Place	Date	Hour	Summary of Events and Information	Remarks and references to Appendices
GOUY-SERVINS Square Q35b Sheet 36B	23rd 24th 25th		Various G.S. wagon fatigues, camp repairs and improvements carried out.	
	26th		48 reinforcements arrived, were posted to 1/Brigades, Trench Mortars, & D.A.C.	
	27th 28th 29th 30th 31st		Various G.S. wagon fatigues carried out by each of the Sections.	

[signatures]

LT. COLONEL R.F.A.
COMMANDING 20th DIVISIONAL AMMUNITION COLUMN

CONFIDENTIAL

Vol 35

WAR DIARY
of
20th Divl. Ammn. Column

from 1st to 30th June 1918

Vol VI

(6392) Wt. W6192/P875 1,500,000 4/18 McA & W Ltd (E 2815) Forms W3091/4.   Army Form W.3091.

Cover for Documents.

Nature of Enclosures.

Notes, or Letters written.

WAR DIARY or INTELLIGENCE SUMMARY

Army Form C. 2118.

June 1918.

Place	Date	Hour	Summary of Events and Information	Remarks and references to Appendices
Headquarters No. 1 and 2 Section GOUY-SERVINS (Q.35A)	5th		Lieut. E.W. AUSTIN, M.C. and party were detailed to proceed by rail to vicinity of BOULOGNE to collect 24 remounts for 20th Divisional Artillery.	R/A.T.
ADLAIN-ST-NAZAIRE (X10A.9)	6th		46 other ranks reinforcements arrived were posted to Brigades and D.A.C.	R/A.T.
No. 3 Section	11th		Lieut. E.W. AUSTIN M.C. and party returned with 66 remounts which were handed over to 32nd mobile Veterinary Section in PETIT SERVINS (Q.35A) Sheet 44B.	R/M.T.
	13th		20 other ranks reinforcements arrived were posted to Brigades and D.A.C.	R/A.T.
	20th		F.G.C.M. assembled at D.A.C., H.Q. for the trial of 45424 Gunner Taylor Z. of No. 3 Section, 20th D.A.C.	R/A.T.
	21st		In accordance with orders of D.D.R. 1st Army (received through 20th D.A.) 60 horses of "A" Echelon	R/A.T.

Army Form C. 2118.

WAR DIARY
or
INTELLIGENCE SUMMARY.   June 1918.

(Erase heading not required.)

Instructions regarding War Diaries and Intelligence Summaries are contained in F. S. Regs., Part II. and the Staff Manual respectively. Title pages will be prepared in manuscript.

Place	Date	Hour	Summary of Events and Information	Remarks and references to Appendices
No. 5 Section AOLAIN-ST-NAZAIRE (X10A18) Headquarters. No 1 and 2 Sections GOUY-SERVINS (Q35Y)			were sent together with 11 horses from Brigade by stages to No. 4 Base Remount Depot at PONT-DE-BRIQUES near BOULOGNE. 20th Divisional Artillery party was under Lieut. E.W. AUSTIN, M.C.	AKS
	22nd		6 other rank reinforcements arrived and were posted to Brigade.	AKS
	27th		A quantity of ammunition was drawn from "C" Army dump (R.7.D.1.4.) Sheet 44B. relivered to calibration range.	AKS
	29th		Party of 18 other ranks British West Indies Regiment arrived there sent to PANET ammunition dump (AOLAIN-ST-NAZAIRE) in relief of British personnel	AKS

Army Form C. 2118.

WAR DIARY
or
INTELLIGENCE SUMMARY.

(Erase heading not required.)

June 1918.

Instructions regarding War Diaries and Intelligence Summaries are contained in F.S. Regs., Part II. and the Staff Manual respectively. Title pages will be prepared in manuscript.

Place	Date	Hour	Summary of Events and Information	Remarks and references to Appendices
Headquarters, No. 1 and 2 Section GOUY-SERVINS (Q.25.d) No. 3 Section ABLAIN-ST-NAZAIRE (X.10.a.O.a.d)	Shell 19		At irregular intervals during the month Officers and other ranks were sent on Trench Mortar and Anti-gas courses. G.S. wagons were turned out daily on various Divisional fatigues. Camp repairs and improvements to particularly the revetting of hose tics (anti-bomb protection) were carried out. Ammunition supply was worked on Deauville system through PANET dump, Lieut A.T.GULLIVER, M.C. in charge. R.H. Denman Capt R.A.	PRS. PRS. PRS. PRS.

R.H. Denman
Capt R.A.
[stamp:] COMMANDING 20th DIVISIONAL AMMUNITION COLUMN
LT. COLONEL R.F.A.

Confidential

WR 36

WAR DIARY.

20th Divnl. Ammn. Column.

from 1st to 31st July. 1918.

Vol VII

(6392) Wt. W6192/P875 1,500,000 4/18 McA & W Ltd (E 2815) Forms W3091/4.   Army Form W.3091

Cover for Documents.

Nature of Enclosures.

Notes, or Letters written.

Army Form C. 2118.

WAR DIARY
or
INTELLIGENCE SUMMARY.
(Erase heading not required.)

July 1918.

Instructions regarding War Diaries and Intelligence Summaries are contained in F. S. Regs., Part II. and the Staff Manual respectively. Title pages will be prepared in manuscript.

Place	Date	Hour	Summary of Events and Information	Remarks and references to Appendices
Headquarters, No. 1 and 2 Sections GOUY-SERVINS (Q35d) Sheet 44B No. 3 Section ABLAIN-ST-NAZAIRE (X10A&B)	2nd		A quantity of ammunition was collected from "B" Army dump (W3B Sheet 44B) removed to PETEWAWA calibration range (X2c Sheet 44B).	Apx D
	7th 8th		17 other ranks reinforcements arrived from 1st Army reinforcement camp were posted to Brigades and D.A.C.	Apx D
	11th		Lt. GIBBARD, and party proceeded to THEROUANNE to collect remounts for 2nd Divisional Artillery	Apx D
	14th		28 other ranks reinforcements arrived from 1st Army reinforcement camp were posted to Brigades, B.A.C. and Trench Mortar Batteries	Apx D
	19th		20 other ranks reinforcements arrived from 1st Army reinforcement camp were posted to Brigades, D.A.C. and Trench Mortar Batteries.	Apx D
	20th		10 other ranks reinforcements arrived from 1st Army reinforcement camp were posted to Brigades and D.A.C.	Apx D

WAR DIARY or INTELLIGENCE SUMMARY

Army Form C. 2118.

July 1918.

Place	Date	Hour	Summary of Events and Information	Remarks and references to Appendices
Headquarters, Nos. 1 and 2 Section, GOUY-SERVINS (Q.35.b) 44B, No. 3 Section ABLAIN-ST-NAZAIRE (X.10.a.a.a.)	25th	11-30 p.m	Vicinity of GOUY-SERVINS was attacked by hostile aircraft. Bombs were dropped in No. 1 Section camp (about W.5.B central Sheet 44B). Casualties to extent of 5 killed and 30 wounded were sustained, the number being in large owing to one bomb bursting in the air on the gable of a house. 18 other ranks reinforcements arrived from 1st Army reinforcement camp were posted to Brigades and D.A.C.	P.M.S.
	27th			P.M.S.
	28th and 29th		A quantity of ammunition was collected from "B" Army dump (W.3.B Sheet 44B) & conveyed to PETEWAWA calibration range (X.2.c Sheet 44B)	P.M.S.

Army Form C. 2118.

WAR DIARY
or
INTELLIGENCE SUMMARY.
(Erase heading not required.)

July 1918.

Place	Date	Hour	Summary of Events and Information	Remarks and references to Appendices

During the whole month ammunition supply was worked on the Decauville System through PANET dump (MOULIN-ST-NAZAIRE) - Lieut A.T. GULLIVER, M.C. in charge. A.S. wagons were turned out daily on various Divisional fatigues.

Camp improvements, repairs, were carried out, also revetting of mens huts, three huts (anti-bomb protection).

Officers and other ranks were sent at regular intervals on Signalling, Anti-Gas, Trench mortar, Lewis Gun Courses.

Appx.

R.H. Bennun
Capt. R.A.
for LT. COLONEL
COMMANDING 20th DIVISIONAL AMMUNITION COLUMN

CONFIDENTIAL

WM 37

WAR DIARY
of
20th DIVL AMMN. COLUMN
from 1st to 31st AUGUST 1918
Vol VIII

(6339) Wt. W160/M3016 1,500,000 10/17 McA & W Ltd (E 1898) Forms W3091.   Army Form W.3091.

Cover for Documents.

Nature of Enclosures.

Notes, or Letters written.

Army Form C. 2118.

WAR DIARY
or
INTELLIGENCE SUMMARY.
(Erase heading not required.)

August 1918.

Instructions regarding War Diaries and Intelligence Summaries are contained in F. S. Regs., Part II. and the Staff Manual respectively. Title pages will be prepared in manuscript.

Place	Date	Hour	Summary of Events and Information	Remarks and references to Appendices
No. 3 Section ADAIN-ST-NAZAIRE (X10 a a 4 B) Gody-SERVINS (Q35Y) Sheet 44B Headquarters, No. 1 and 2 Sections	2nd		2/Lieut. LAMBERT and party proceeded to THEROUANNE to collect remounts for 20th Divisional Artillery.	F.W.K
	3rd		A quantity of ammunition was collected from "B" Army dump (W 3 B Sheet 44B) & conveyed to PETE WANA calibration range (X 2 c Sheet 44B).	F.W.K
	4th		31 other ranks reinforcements arrived from 1st Army reinforcement camp & were posted to Brigades & D.A.C.	F.W.K
	6th		F.G.C.M. assembled at D.A.C. Headquarters for the trial of Gunner Clarke G. of No. 3 Section.	F.W.K
	10th		27 other ranks reinforcements arrived from 1st Army reinforcement camp & were posted to Brigades, Trench Mortars & D.A.C.	F.W.K
	12th		9 other ranks reinforcements arrived from 1st Army	F.W.K

WAR DIARY
or
INTELLIGENCE SUMMARY

Army Form C. 2118.

(Erase heading not required.)

Place	Date	Hour	Summary of Events and Information	Remarks and references to Appendices
No. 3 Section ABLAIN-ST-NAZAIRE (X10a0.8)	18th		reinforcement camp & were posted to French Mortars. 6 other ranks reinforcements arrived from 1st Army reinforcement camp & were posted to Brigades.	Pkt 5
	23rd		2/Lieut. GIBBARD and party proceeded to THEROUANNE to collect returns for 20th Divisional Artillery	Pkt 5
	26th		F.G.C.M. assembled at D.A.C. Headquarters for the trial of Gunner Habgood of No. 2 Section.	Pkt 5
			During the whole month the ammunition supply was worked on the Deauville system through PANET dump (ABLAIN-ST-NAZAIRE) - Lieut. E. BARKER in charge until relieved by 2/Lieut. H. GILBERT.	Pkt 5

(P.T.O.)

Headquarters, No. 1 and 2 Sections
GOUY-SERVINS (Q35D)

Sept

WAR DIARY
or
INTELLIGENCE SUMMARY.

August 1918.

Army Form C. 2118.

Place	Date	Hour	Summary of Events and Information	Remarks and references to Appendices
			G.S. wagons were turned out daily on various Divisional fatigues. Camp improvements & repairs to wire huts & stables were carried out. Officers and other ranks were sent at regular intervals on Anti-gas, Trench Mortar, Lewis Gun and Indian Courses.	R.K.S. R.K.S. R.K.S. R.K.S.

R.H. Denman Capt ?

LT. COLONEL
COMMANDING 20th DIVISIONAL AMMUNITION ?

CONFIDENTIAL

Vol 38

WAR DIARY
of
20th Divl. Ammn. Column
from 1st to 30th Sept 1918
Vol IX

(6339) Wt. W160/M3016 1,500,000 10/17 McA & W Ltd (E 1898) Forms W3091.   Army Form W.3091.

Cover for Documents.

Nature of Enclosures.

Notes, or Letters written.

Army Form C. 2118.

WAR DIARY
or
INTELLIGENCE SUMMARY.
(Erase heading not required.)

September 1918.

Headquarters No. 1 and 2 Sections Silchip
No. 3 Section ABLAIN-ST-NAZAIRE (X10A0w3)
Gouy-SERVINS (O35)

Place	Date	Hour	Summary of Events and Information	Remarks and references to Appendices
	6th		A quantity of road revetting camouflage was drawn from DUISANS (N.W. of ARRAS) and delivered to R.E. dump at LENS JUNCTION.	J.J.A.S.
		10th	Party of Lieut. E.W.AUSTIN, M.C. 2 N.C.O's + 50 other ranks proceeded to PANET ammunition dump & travelled up an ammunition train to M30 c 6-2 (refer. map. ST. NAZAIRE and trench map.) At this spot 3600 rounds 18 pdr. ammn. was unloaded + conveyed to forward positions at M36A75.90 and M36 B 0.9 respectively. In these positions ammn. was carefully stacked + camouflaged.	J.J.A.S.
	15th		Gotha raids reinforcements arrived from 1st Army reinforcement camp + were posted to 91st Brigade B.J.A.	J.B.J.A.

WAR DIARY
or
INTELLIGENCE SUMMARY.

(Erase heading not required.)

Army Form C. 2118.

September 1918.

Place	Date	Hour	Summary of Events and Information	Remarks and references to Appendices
Headquarters, Nos. 1 and 2 Sections Gouy SERVINS (O35d) Sheet 44B No. 3 Section AGLAIN-ST-NAZAIRE (X10A04B)	29th		33 other ranks reinforcements arrived from 1st Army reinforcement camp were posted to Brigades and D.A.C.	R.S.
			During the whole month the ammunition was worked on the Deauville Railway system though PANET dump, 2/Lt. H. GILBERT and 2/Lt. F. DOBSON in charge. Quantities of ry. were drawn by lorry and wagons from FOSSE 9 (O9c) Sheet 44B even for making roads & repairing horse standings in Section camps. Various camp repairs & improvements were effected G.S. wagons were turned out daily in various Divisional fatigues. Officers and other ranks were sent on Indoor, Trench Mortar, & Anti-gas courses.	R.S. R.S. R.S.

P.N. O'Connor
Lt Colonel R.F.A.
Commanding 20th Divisional Ammunition Column

CONFIDENTIAL

WAR DIARY
of
20th DIVL. AMM. COLUMN
from 1st to 31st October 1918
Vol X

98/39

(6339) Wt. W160/M3016 1,500,000 10/17 McA & W Ltd (E 1898) Forms W3091. Army Form W.3091.

Cover for Documents.

Nature of Enclosures.

Notes, or Letters written.

WAR DIARY or INTELLIGENCE SUMMARY

Army Form C. 2118.

October 1918.

Place	Date	Hour	Summary of Events and Information	Remarks and references to Appendices
HQ. No. 1 and 2 Sections at GOUY-SERVINS. No. 3 Section at ABLAIN-ST-NAZAIRE. Subsequently lines of march subsequently shop L.F.N.S. 17.	1st to 5th		Various G.S. wagon fatigues carried out including work at PETEWAWA (Siberian) Range (ABLAIN ST NAZAIRE)	Pers
	4th		Ammunition was salvaged from special forward position taken to PANET Ammunition dump (ABLAIN-ST-NAZAIRE)	Pers
	6th		No. 3 Section marched out to CAMBLIGNEUL came under orders of 20th Division "Q."	Pers
	7th		Headquarters Nos. 1 and 2 Sections, on relief by 50th D.A.C., marched out from GOUY-SERVINS proceeded via VILLERS-AU-BOIS and MONT-ST-ELOY to ARRAS billetted for night	Pers
	8th		at ARRAS awaiting orders	Pers
	9th		Marched via ARRAS and GUEMAPPE and camped between CHERISY and VIS-EN-ARTOIS.	Pers

WAR DIARY
or
INTELLIGENCE SUMMARY.

Army Form C. 2118.

October 1918.

Place	Date	Hour	Summary of Events and Information	Remarks and references to Appendices
VIS-EN-ARTOIS Reserve Camp Jefferies Camp 2 CHERISY Reserve Camp LENS II	10th		Headquarters D.A.C. moved into SUN QUARRY camp on CHERISY-HENDECOURT road.	Rons
	13th		122 remounts drawn from ARAAS recirculated in DAC lines until handed over to 57th Divl. Artillery at RAMILLIES CHURCH (N.E. of CAMBRAI).	Rons
	15th		240 remounts drawn from ARAAS recirculated in DAC lines until handed over to 39th and 49th Divl. Artillery	Rons
	25th		31 remounts drawn from ARAAS recirculated in DAC lines until handed over to 52nd A.F.A. Brigade.	Rons
	26th		48 remounts for 4th Divl. Arty., 41 remounts for 39th Divl Arty., 24 remounts for 49th Divl Arty., and 40 remounts for 2nd A.F.A. Bde drawn from ARAAS recirculated	Rons

WAR DIARY
or
INTELLIGENCE SUMMARY.
(Erase heading not required.)

Army Form C. 2118.

October 1918.

Place	Date	Hour	Summary of Events and Information	Remarks and references to Appendices
			an D.A.C. lines with headed road at RAMILLIES CHURCH. Ammunition & water to 158 Cy. A.S.C. trains H.D. removed.	Ros
	28th		40 rounds for SW.D.W. Arty. 39 rounds for 175th MA Brigade drawn from M.T.R.A.S. recannalised in DAC R315. Lines with headed road at RAMILLIES CHURCH. During the period 10th to 30th October whilst the Sections were bivouaced on the CHERISY-VIS-EN-ARTOIS road extensive salvage work was carried out and a large area surrounding the camps. A quantity small arms ammunition, various stores, equipment & unreadable R.E. material was salved, roughly in a	R315 Ros

WAR DIARY
INTELLIGENCE SUMMARY.

Army Form C. 2118.

October 1918.

Place	Date	Hour	Summary of Events and Information	Remarks and references to Appendices
	30th		Further movement to the Decauville Rly. system.	Pers.
			H.Q. Nos 1 and 2 Sections worked from CHERISY via VIS-EN-ARTOIS and MARQUION to CAMBRAI billetted in barracks in that town.	Pers.
	31st		At CAMBRAI awaiting orders.	
			Move on the 30th from CHERISY was consequent upon transfer of 20th Divl. artillery from 1st to 3rd Army.	Pers.

R.J. Dennison Capt MA
for LT. COLONEL
COMMANDING 20th DIVISIONAL AMMUNITION.

CONFIDENTIAL

98/40

War Diary
of
20th Divnl. Ammn. Column.

From 1.11.18 to 30.11.18

Vol: XI.

(6392) Wt. W6192/P875 1,500,000 4/18 McA & W Ltd (E 2815) Forms W3091/4.   Army Form W.3091.

Cover for Documents.

Nature of Enclosures.

Notes, or Letters written.

Army Form C. 2118.

WAR DIARY
or
INTELLIGENCE SUMMARY.
(Erase heading not required.)

November 1918.

Instructions regarding War Diaries and Intelligence Summaries are contained in F. S. Regs., Part II. and the Staff Manual respectively. Title pages will be prepared in manuscript.

Place	Date	Hour	Summary of Events and Information	Remarks and references to Appendices
Barracks in CAMBRAI and later French Trench	1st		No. 3 Section having entrained in back area arrived in CAMBRAI and billeted, but received marching orders of 20th Div. "Q". H.Q. 20th D.A.C. Nos. 1 and 2 Sections in barracks CAMBRAI awaiting orders.	/L
	2nd		H.Q. Nos. 1 and 2 Sections marched to vicinity of SAULZOIR about P33B Sheet 51A ready for the night.	/L
	3rd		H.Q. Nos. 1 and 2 Sections marched thence on road about Q7D between SOMMAING and VENDEGIES. Sections immediately commenced supply of ammunition to batteries of 91st and 92nd Bdes.	/L
	6th		H.Q. Nos. 1 and 2 Sections marched thence, billeted in and near VILLERS-POL in Square L34 Sheet 51A, to facilitate supply of ammunition to batteries.	/L

Army Form C. 2118.

WAR DIARY
or
INTELLIGENCE SUMMARY.
(Erase heading not required.)

November 1918.

Instructions regarding War Diaries and Intelligence Summaries are contained in F. S. Regs., Part II. and the Staff Manual respectively. Title pages will be prepared in manuscript.

Place	Date	Hour	Summary of Events and Information	Remarks and references to Appendices
Line of March	7th		H.Q. Nos. 1 and 2 Sections marched billets in WARGNIES-LE-GRAND in square G.15.c Sheet 51.	
	8th		H.Q. Nos. 1 and 2 Sections marched billets = about X roads in square H.20.c Sheet 51.	
	9th		H.Q. and No. 2 Section marched billets in BREAUGIES area about H.17.B Sheet 51. No.1 Section remained in billets about H.20.c. (Up till this date the Column has about daily pushed forward maintaining close touch with batteries thus ensuring prompt delivery of ammunition. Dumps were cleared as the Column went forward.	
	10th		Awaiting orders.	
	11th		Orders received from 20th Artillery Headquarters that Column would remain in billets until further instructions.	

Army Form C. 2118.

WAR DIARY
or
INTELLIGENCE SUMMARY.
(Erase heading not required.)

November 1918.

Place	Date	Hour	Summary of Events and Information	Remarks and references to Appendices
	1st		H.Q. and No. 2 Section at BREAUGIES (H17D Sheet 51) and No. 1 Section at X roads to West of Wood (H20c Sheet 51). This period was occupied in turn over of ammunition in echelon, repair returning of wagons etc etc.	
	2nd			
	22nd		H.Q. Nos 1 and 2 Sections received orders from 20th Artillery H.Q. marched at ORSINVAL (Square R11B Sheet 51A)	
	23rd		At ORSINVAL.	
	24th		Marched from ORSINVAL via RUESNES, BERMERAIN and Chaussee Brunehalt road to CAMBRAI billetted in Cavalry Barracks in that town where 20th Artillery was concentrated	
	27th		Marched from CAMBRAI via Cambrai-Bapaume road to vicinity of FAVREUIL occupied camps near that place for the night.	

Army Form C. 2118.

WAR DIARY
or
INTELLIGENCE SUMMARY.
(Erase heading not required.)

November 1918.

Place	Date	Hour	Summary of Events and Information	Remarks and references to Appendices
POMMIER (Sheet LENS 11)	28th		Marched from vicinity of FAIREUIL in Achiet-le-Grand, le Petit, Bucquoy & Hannescamps to POMMIER (rest area see Sheet LENS 11)	
	29th and 30th		at POMMIER.	

Lambert
Lt. Colonel R.F.A.
Commanding 20th Divisional Ammunition Column

Confidential.

Vol 4!

War Diary
of
20th Divisional Ammn. Col.

From: 1.12.18. To 31.12.18.

Vol. 12.

(6392) Wt. W6192/P875 1,500,000 4/18 McA & W Ltd (E 2815) Forms W3091/4. Army Form W.3091.

Cover for Documents.

Nature of Enclosures.

Notes, or Letters written.

Army Form C. 2118.

WAR DIARY
or
INTELLIGENCE SUMMARY.
(Erase heading not required.)

December 1918.

Place	Date	Hour	Summary of Events and Information	Remarks and references to Appendices
H.Q. No. 1 and 2 Sections POMMIER No. 3 Section WARLINCOURT Refes Shock ENGIN.			Early part of month was devoted to experiments in new kilns in brass, & bone shavings & tables. In this work, assistance was obtained from R.E.'s also a P.O.W. working party. Educational Scheme was organized in Bde. & classes held in recreation room. Periodical football matches, various army indoor sports held in accordance with Divisional scheme for recreational training of troops. The latter part of the month, the cool weather in the Clerk were dispatched to CAMBRAI for demobilization according to their different centres. Hamilton LT. COLONEL R.F.A. COMMANDING 20th DIVISIONAL AMMUNITION COLUMN	#

Wd 42

War Diary

of

20th Divnl. Ammunition Column.

From : 1st Jan. 1919.

To : 31st Jan. 1919.

Vol: I.

CONFIDENTIAL

(6392) Wt. W6192/P875 1,500,000 4/18 McA & W Ltd (E 2815) Forms W3091/4.   Army Form W.3091.

Cover for Documents.

Nature of Enclosures.

Notes, or Letters written.

Army Form C. 2118.

WAR DIARY
or
INTELLIGENCE SUMMARY.
(Erase heading not required.)

January 1919

Place	Date	Hour	Summary of Events and Information	Remarks and references to Appendices
H.Q. & Nos. 1 and 2 Sections, POMMIER. No. 3 Section, WARLINCOURT. Rifle Shoot LENS II.			Lectures and Classes have been held daily throughout the month on the following subjects:- History, Mathematics, French, Account and Bookkeeping, Carpentry & Blacksmith duties etc. etc. Physical Training programme has been carried out during the month and indoor Sports held in the evenings. As circumstances permitted, Trench filling was carried out in the vicinity of POMMIER, and a total of 560 yds filled in - in the vicinity of Section Camps and Walcz Tnorights POMMIER. Unboxed Ammunition was removed by Nos. 1 and 2 Sects from Salvage Dump POMMIER and taken to Salvage dump at PAS - 500 yds from PAS on MONDICOURT Rd.	✗ ✗ ✗

WAR DIARY
or
INTELLIGENCE SUMMARY.
(Erase heading not required.)

Army Form C. 2118.

January 1919.

Place	Date	Hour	Summary of Events and Information	Remarks and references to Appendices
	26th		A party of 3 Officers and 45 men proceeded to CANDAS to staff the 3rd Army Animal Collecting Camp	
			103 Horses were dispatched to No 3 Base Remount Depot on 14th inst and 72 Mules and 9 Horses dispatched to TOURNAI on 31st	
			During the month of January No 3 Section have turned out on an average 8 Wagons + Teams per day for Divisional Fatigues, etc.	
			A Total of 1 Officer and 43 other ranks have been demobilized in the month	

Ferdub
LT. COLONEL, R.F.A.
COMMANDING 25th DIVISIONAL AMMUNITION COLUMN.

8843

War Diary
of
20th Divnl. Ammunition Col.

From: 1:2:19.
To: 28:2:19.

Vol: 2.

CONFIDENTIAL

(6392) Wt. W6192/P875 1,500,000 4/18 McA & W Ltd (E 2815) Forms W3091/4.   Army Form W.3091.

Cover for Documents.

Nature of Enclosures.

Notes, or Letters written.

Army Form C. 2118.

WAR DIARY
or
INTELLIGENCE SUMMARY.
(Erase heading not required.)

Instructions regarding War Diaries and Intelligence Summaries are contained in F. S. Regs., Part II. and the Staff Manual respectively. Title pages will be prepared in manuscript.

February 1919.

Place	Date	Hour	Summary of Events and Information	Remarks and references to Appendices
H.Q., H/os 1 and 2 Sections. POMMIER H/o 3 Section. WARLINCOURT Style Sheet LENS II.			Extensive Salvage work was carried out during the month, Ammunition, Charges, Cartridge cases etc., being collected from Salvage dump St AMAND Street, POMMIER and also from billets in POMMIER and taken to RAILHEAD, MONDICOURT. Periodical football matches & indoor evening sports held in accordance with Divisional scheme for recreational training of troops. Educational Classes held in recreation rooms. During the month 1 Officer and 22 other ranks were despatched to dispersal areas for demobilisation. Whilst on leave in U.K. 30 other ranks were demobilised.	※ ※ ※ ※

WAR DIARY
INTELLIGENCE SUMMARY

February 1919.

Army Form C. 2118.

Place	Date	Hour	Summary of Events and Information	Remarks and references to Appendices
HQ 1 and 2 Sections POMMIER / 3 Section WARLINCOURT / Regt Sheet LENS 11.	6th 16th 17th		6 other ranks volunteered for one year's service with the Armies of Occupation under A.O. XIV of Jan 29. 1919. All Ammunition in charge of R.A.6 was taken to OZ Ammunition Railhead, FIENVILLERS, where it was dumped and receipts obtained	
	14th		Following "Y" horses despatched to CANDAS – 3 L.D. and 1 Rdg. 21 "Z" L.D. horses and 3 "Z" Mules despatched to 32nd M.V.S	
GRINCOURT	24th		2 "X" Mules handed over to Camp Commdt PAS.	
	28th		3 "D" animals sent to 30th M.V.S. CAMBRAI.	

[signature]
Capt R.F.A.

[signature]
Lt. Colonel R.F.A.

WAR DIARY
or
INTELLIGENCE SUMMARY.
(Erase heading not required.)

Army Form C. 2118.

March 1919

Place	Date	Hour	Summary of Events and Information	Remarks and references to Appendices
HQ and 1 & 2 Sections POMMIER / #3 Section WARLINCOURT Ref Sheet LENS 11	10th		10 Indian Reinforcements arrived from Base Depot ROUEN and posted to Sections of D.A.C.	
	12th		Under orders from 20th Div Arty, all surplus Stores & harness, etc, was packed in G.S. Wagons and taken to Gun Park, MONDICOURT, together with R.A. Wagons of Nos 1 and 2 Sections	
	15th		Stores of D.I.M.O. 20th Division, were packed in G.S. Wagons of No. 3 Section and packed as above. Guard of 8 Men, under 2/Lt 1070.5 Gibbons was found by Sections for duty at the Gun Park, MONDICOURT.	
	25th		1 Sgt and 10 Drivers (returnable) were despatched to 2nd Army Reinforcement Camp for posting to 41st D.A.	

WAR DIARY
or
INTELLIGENCE SUMMARY.

Army Form C. 2118.

March 1919

Place	Date	Hour	Summary of Events and Information	Remarks and references to Appendices
H.Q. and 1 and 2 Sections, POMMIER. No. 3 Section WARLINCOURT, Ref. Sheet, LENS 11	28th		The Indians attached to #Qrs - Nos 1 + 2 Sections joined No. 3, WARLINCOURT, billets being found for the whole of the Indian personnel by O.C. No 3 Section	7D
	29th		8 pair Wheelers provided to remove transport of 2nd 8 R. from Wagon Park MONDICOURT to CANDAS. During the month, horses + mules have been despatched to Collecting Camps, etc as under:-	9D
			To 3rd Army A.E.C. CANDAS - 42 horses do - to entrain for 2nd Army 76 Mules To XVII Corps A.E.C. BEAUVAL - 50 horses + 2 Mules To 19th V.E.S. DOULLENS - 3 horses - 98 Mules.	7D 7D

Cont'd

Army Form C. 2118.

WAR DIARY
or
INTELLIGENCE SUMMARY.
(Erase heading not required.)

March 1919

Place	Date	Hour	Summary of Events and Information	Remarks and references to Appendices
			To 32nd M.V.S. GRINCOURT — 6 Horses — 90 Mules	
			To 31st M.V.S. BERNAVILLE — 10 Mules.	
			Owing to shortage of Animals fatigues to be done by batteries, 8 Mules were transferred to 91st Bde R.F.A.	
			Capt. H.W. AUSTIN (CF) and Lieut. H.J.L. KENDALL (R.F.A.) and 42 Other Ranks were despatched to CANDAS for dispersal during the month.	
			30 other ranks demobilized whilst on leave to U.K.	
			5 Regulars proceeded on furlough to U.K. on 28th March.	

F. Pirro
2/Lt. R.F.A.
LT. COLONEL R.F.A.
COMMANDING 20th DIVISIONAL AMMUNITION COLUMN

20 D Am Col
April 1919
Army Form C. 2118.

WAR DIARY
or
INTELLIGENCE SUMMARY
(Erase heading not required.)

Place	Date	Hour	Summary of Events and Information	Remarks and references to Appendices
JR Cul 1 o 2 Sections c/o 3 Section WARLINGCOURT Rly Shed LENS II	3rd		Capt Heather RAV (Royal Books) DJMO 20th Division, attached to No 3 Section, proceeded on leave to UK	
	5th		Capt AJ Gulliver RFA proceeded on leave to UK, Lt Gilbert taking over command of No 3 Section (temporary)	
POMMIER	6th		Lt White ST attached 14th Corps A.C.C. granted 14 days leave to UK	
	"		All X Animals sent to BEAUVAL and exchanged for Z Animals	
	8th		6 other ranks posted to 2nd Army RFA Reinforcement Camp	
	9th		Lieut A Gilbert RFA posted to 2nd Army – to 2/Lt Tarrant JR taking No 3 Section over until posted to 2nd Army	

WAR DIARY
or
INTELLIGENCE SUMMARY.
(Erase heading not required.)

Army Form C. 2118.

April 1918.

Place	Date	Hour	Summary of Events and Information	Remarks and references to Appendices
	10th		Under orders received from 20th Divl. Arty., the following Officers & personnel were detailed for duty with "Z" Horse Depot. "A" Squadron forming at GEZAINCOURT - Capt J.A Codner. R.M. 150 Natives O.R's and 1 Batman. "B" Squadron forming at WARLINCOURT. On departure of Capt J.A Codner, 2/Lieut F. Dobson took Command of No. 2 Section.	/ / /
	11th		2/Lt Savant F.L. posted to 2nd Army Reinforcement Camp. 2/Lt Gebbard W.W.S taking command of No 3 Section until return of Capt A.T. Gullies from leave.	/

WAR DIARY
INTELLIGENCE SUMMARY

April 1919

Army Form C. 2118.

Place	Date	Hour	Summary of Events and Information	Remarks and references to Appendices
	15th		146 Horses & Mules transferred to No 3 Section from 91st Bde. R.F.A.	
	21st		Capt A.T. Gulliver having returned from leave, takes over command of No 3 Section - 2/Lt Gibbard M.M.G.S returning to No 1 Section for duty. During the whole of the month, assistance has been given to the local farmers to fill in trenches & shell craters, chiefly in the vicinity of POMMIER. 2/Lt J. Mason Burton R.F.A and 11 O.R's were sent to CANDAS for dispersal during the month. 2 O.R's demobilised at ...	

Hawkins
Capt. R.F.A.
LT. COLONEL R.F.A.
COMMANDING 20th DIVISIONAL AMMUNITION COLUMN

S.O.
20th Divl M.T. Coy

Herewith List of Honours & Awards as applied to Headquarters and Nos 1 and 3 Sections.

The D.A.C. is comprised of H.Q and only 3 Sections. In Jan/1917, old No 3 Section became 93rd Bde Ammn Col., their No 4 Section became No 3 Section from that time.

Lambert
Capt. R.F.A.
Adjutant

4/19

20th Division.

D.A.C., F.M.,
~~Division~~,
~~A.V.C.~~,
~~Div. ~~~~

O.E

2 O D A.C

St Barbara
I have written to
Col Foster to get a letter
effort from No 2 Sec.

It is very much regretted that the question of compiling a short history of this Unit for insertion in the 20° Divisional History had not been considered before.

It is feared that it is now too late to do so because all the Officers N.C.O's & men of any length of service in the Unit have been demobilized and therefore it is impossible to collect all the detail that would be essential to enable satisfaction and real justice to be done to the effort that should be made. It is therefore decided that nothing can be added to the records contained in the War Diary and it is only desired to add the names of the following Officers and N.C.O's who were serving in this Unit at the time they were awarded for gallantry in the Field:-

<u>Military Cross</u>

CAPT A.T. GULLIVER (then Lieut)
LIEUT E.W. AUSTIN.

Dear McGowan,

I enclose a few papers which may help you in your work. I have had many other testimonials of all sorts of work done by D.A.C. which I did not think worth while keeping but from those enclosed concerning the Pelehem punch, gives a fair test of the working & efficiency of the D.A.C. under most trying circumstances. During the whole of the campaign D.A.C. supplied Am[muniti]on & material to Batteries direct except in the Lens area where this was done by Dreauville R?— Am[muniti]on supplied in the Somme Advance — Pelehem & Parchend[ael] Cambrai Offensive — Amiens Retreats &

final advance, amounting to
1,367000 rounds of gun & [small?].
Mostly done by Nos 1 & 2 Sections
as No 3 was invariably under Cl
for operations. I have to go to No 3
this afternoon so regret I won't be
here to meet you but with these papers
& his diary I think you will be able
to compile the necessary yarn.
Please return the letters etc.

Yrs sincerely
C.W. Foster

DAC was formed about 15th Jany 15
Lt. Col. J R Wortin RHA in Command
Temp Captain P Belcher RHA adjt
2 trumpt'rs
1 Q. M. S.
1 Art'y Clerk
8 Corpls
2 Rou[gh] R[ider]s

300 Men — Civilians

DAC was not made up to its full Strength
in men & horses, until May 15

All the men had to be taught first line
Riding & driving – feeding of horses &
Stable management

Bee tn 28th July 15 the DAC entrained at
Salisbury Plain to embark at Southampton
a complete working unit.

Sect. Comdrs Captains Temp Capt Brookes
" " Robinson
" Henderson

97

D.A.C.

3 section at beginning
Then 4. Then 4 again
One went away with 93rd
N° 3 S.A. Sec under Q for operations
  Then back to R.A.
Indians joined at Cambrai

D.A.C. 3 reg. trunks, div. who had reg. Q.M.; 1 reg R.A clerk.
  been sent home comp. etc
  formed on 15/1/15 at Deepcut.
  300 civilians. Some inj. vics. Horse unit – no seats

Col Cliff Inglefield (Landule)

Inspected (Salisbury Plain) for France
by Gen
Davies   On the 22/7/15 arrived at
Inspected by K of K Harve + Slates Lane
Inspected by Sir F. ?   Day for Jumbos.

Bomb section (N°3) S.A.H.
Verey lights, grenades, stokes mortars

D.A.C. men working in O.P.s Building O.P.s

Officers of D.A.C. reinforced R.A. batteries.
_____

Pack animal work in the Somme
    Great admiration of the Divs
_____

R.E. work. D.A.C. always at work.
_____

Almost every move by march route.
    Only once by train.
_____

One man frozen to death marching
    from Saurgeaumont to Robecq
in June.
_____

Headquarters

Lt. Col. J. R. Foster. R.F.A.	"Mention" Oct/16
Captain R. H. Denman. R.F.A.	"M.C" YPRES 1917

No 1 Section

	Capt. W. P. Hamilton. R.F.A.	"Special Mention" YPRES. campaign 1917.
	Lieut. E. E. Barker. R.F.A.	— do —
68382	B.S.M. Ward J.P.	M.S.M. in connection with SOMME campaign 1916
73573	Sgt Cundy. A.	D.C.M. YPRES 1917
43646	Sgt White J.	M.M. — do —
70137	Sgt Burrill W.	M.S.M. in connection with ST. QUENTIN. retirement 1918
80524	Driver Marson G.	M.M. in connection with VILLERS-BRETTONEUX
	Lieut E. ELLIOTT	M.C. in connection with YPRES campaign Oct/17

No 3 Section

Capt A. T. Gulliver R.F.A.   "M.C."   Oct/17

83916	Cpl Coveney G.	"D.C.M"	YPRES	1916
84055	Cpl Williams A.	"M.M."	AMIENS	1918
69878	Bdr Tatchell A.	"MM"	YPRES	1917
3341	Bdr Harpham M.	"M.M"	AMIENS	1918
10326	Driver Lythgoe R.	"MM"	YPRES	1917

Officers of D.A.C. during Campaign

Commanding for whole period of war.

Lt Colonel J. R. Foster RFA

Adjutants — Captain Belcher RFA
" Denman MC
" Lambert "

Cavalry Sections —

No 1. Sect: Captain Brooke RFA
" Stansbydale "
" Ross Brown "
" Wright "
" Beresford Peirse "
" Hamilton "

No 2. Sect: Captain Robinson RFA
" Cosens "

No 3. Sect: Captain Henderson RFA
" Laing MC "
" McDonald "
" Pollock MC "

On reorganisation No 3 became No 4 Section
& No 3. was commanded by Captain Walker.
+ further reorganisation 93rd Bde became Army Brigade
+ this No 3 section went with it as Bde Amm. Coln
+ No 4 section became again No 3 section carrying S.A.A.
only

+ was invariably under Q branch for all active operations but under D.A.G. for administration + discipline.

                        attached
M.O. i/c - Captain ~~Arkwright~~ Arkwright - R.A.M.C.
   "   Johnson   "
   "   Wall   "
   Lt.   Zinkann   U.S.A
   Captain   Swift   Australian

Vet Officers - Lt. Corden R.A.V.C.
               Capt. Simson R.A.V.C.

Chaplains - Revd. McIntyre C.F.
           "   Warren Austin C.F.

Interpreters - Monsieur Le Blon - Belgian
              "   Richet   French
              "   Gurnot   French

The quality of the personnel was exceedingly good — Men who had volunteered for the war. Determined to see the thing through never spared themselves under all the varying conditions of warfare Shewing the greatest devotion to duty & never failing in their tasks on the most difficult occasions. Through the good & sound principles inculcated by Br. Genl. John Stokham C.B. the 1st C.R.A. of the 20th D.H. the 20th D.A.C. maintained throughout the Campaign a good reputation for the Condition of its horses & mules, the horsemastership of the various Section Comdrs. left nothing to be desired —

L W Foster Lt. Col. N.Z.A.
Comdg 20th D.A.C.

20th Divisional Ammunition Column R.F.A.

Casualties (16)

Regtl No	Rank	Name	Remarks
70185	Dr	Houghton E.	Admitted to Hosptl 24.12.15. Died in No 2. London C.C.S. Buried in Merville Cemetery 25-12-15.
101149	Gr	Vincent T.	Wounded in Action 16-3-16
65655	-	Lovesay A.E.	do "
83977	Dr	Samson E.	do "
101149	Gr	Vincent T. ✗	Died of Wounds rec'd in Action 16-3-16
97092	Dr	Hasty A.V. ✗	Killed in Action 16-3-16. Buried in FERME OLLIVER Cemetery. Map Sheet 28. B.13.b.6.5.
65655	Gr	Lovesay A.E.	Died of wounds rec'd in action 17/3/16
83977	Dr	Samson E.	Buried in Soldiers Cemetery — 18/3/16. Sheet 27 L.22.d.6.3.
110052	Gr	Maughan T.	Wounded in Action 19-3-16. To England 6.4.16
121159	"	Witts E.	Killed in Action whilst att to C/91. 7-6-16. Buried, Prison Cemetery. YPRES Sheet 28 I.Y. Central.
122672	Gr	Browning J.G.	Wounded in Action, att to C/91. 7-6-16
2/35610	Dr	Elwood H.	Died from Myelitis Diffuse 15-6-16
21677	Gr	Molloy P.	Wounded in Action 18-6-16. Died of Wounds rec'd in Action 19-6-16. Buried Cemetery LISSENHOEK Sheet 27 L.22.D.6.3.
83143	Dr	Bedingfield A.	Wounded in Action 26-6-16
112390	"	Jones T.	do
54480	Gr	Starris F.	do 30-6-16
109626	"	West A.G.	do "
32315	-	Schofield S.	do "
46294	Dr	Harman T.	Wounded in Action 29-6-16
94139	"	Swan G.	do 30-6-16
70202	Dr	Neish R.	Wounded in Action 5-10-16. Died from Wounds rec'd in Action - Buried CARNOY Mil. Cemy. 1½ miles W of MARICOURT

100100	Dr	Collins T.	Wounded in Action	5.10.16
41423	"	Morgan T.	Killed in Action	7.10.16
79638	Gr	Dempsey F.G.	- do -	- do -
18873	Dr	Laverick J.	Wounded in Action	22-11-16
97520	S/S	Baker E.	Buried in St Sever Cemetery extension ROUEN GRAND, QUEVILLY.	
18301	Dr	Gorman P.	Wounded in Action	31-12-16
80281	"	Salter S.	Killed in Action Buried GINCHY. N.W of COMBLES.	31-12-16
70130	Dr	Corless J.	Died from Heart Failure Buried at CARNOY Cemetery	24-12-16
99163	Farr Sgt	Chinn H.	Wounded in Action	3-12-17
159090	Gr	Scarborough MAL	✗ Wounded in Action	30-11-17
206570	"	Miles W	- do - do -	" " "
159090	Gr	Scarborough MAL	✗ Died of Wounds	3-12-17
169600	Gr	Nisbet G.	Wounded in Action	30-11-17
184448	Dr	Sullivan J.	- do -	6-11-17
43448	Gr	Canton W	- do -	16-9-17
70424	Dr	Howarth W.H.	- do - Died from Wounds recd in Action	23-8-17 16-9-17
37359	Dr	Davies J.	Killed in Action	11-9-17
37340	"	Jones D.J.	- do -	- do -
41430	Dr	Davies A.S.	Wounded in Action	11-9-17
70467	"	Williamson C.	- do -	12-9-17
191846	"	Hawley F.W.	- do - "Gassed"	12-9-17
114101	Dr	Fatkins F.M.	Killed in Action	5-9-17
43660	"	Phillips W.J.	- do -	5-9-17
83468	S/S	Gillion H.	Wounded in Action	16-8-17
83164	Bdr	Hewson C.	- do -	19-8-17
70510	Dr	Johnson C.	- do -	16-8-17
69461	Sgt	Bown C.	- do -	17-8-17
54121	Dr	Burton H.	- do -	17-8-17
161216	Dr	Hoyle T.	Killed in Action	10-8-17
94924	Sdlr Cpl	Belair E.	Wounded in Action	11-8-17
229038	Gr	Walker E.E.	- do -	15-8-17
11860	Dr	Huggins W.J.	- do -	14-8-17

L/30196	Gr	Darlaw A.E.	Killed in Action	29.7.17
54531	Bdr	Gliddon J.C.	- do -	28.7.17
177728	a/Bdr	Hudson G.	- do -	28.7.17
86534	Dr	Hopkins C.H.	Died from Wounds rec'd in Action	29.7.17
70269	Dr	Forshaw H.	Killed in Action	27.7.17
224229	"	Fensom A.	- do -	27.7.17
110879	"	Reacord J.	- do -	27.7.17
70210	"	Thompson L.	- do -	22.7.17
43421	Cpl	Ebbege G.	Wounded in Action	21.7.17
L/1340	Dr	Morgan G.	do	"
109908	Gr	Walker J.	do	"
72398	Dr	Ross W.E.	do	23.7.17
70845	.	Dear J.	do	
83328	Gr	Cundy A.	do	20.7.17
82092	Cpl	Martin A.	do	24.7.17
70366	Dr	Sharrock F.	do	23.7.17
168693	Gr	Purchese E.	do	" " "
95953	Dr	Rathbone R.	do	20.7.17
20646	-	Smith A.	do	21.7.17
54532	Dr	Cole J.	do	- -
96970	"	Tease W.	do	22.7.17
98022	a/Bdr	Talbot J.R.	do	23.7.17
201460	Dr	Callear A.	do	20.7.17
198499	"	Dunn J.	do	21.7.17
54457	-	Bailey C.H.	do	21.7.17
80632	Gr	Stapleton J.	do	17.7.17
52734	S/S	Berry R.J.	do	18.7.17
46399	Dr	Miller A.	do	18.7.17
83925	Gr	Hardy J.A.	do	18.7.17
70641	Dr	Singleton T.	do "Gassed"	- do -
107825	Dr	Hartnell Geo	do "Gassed"	- do -
156167	Gr	Wildish G.W.	Died from Pneumonia 26.3.17. Buried Grove Town Brit. Mil. Cemetery Sheet 62D. - F25 c 3 9	
19739	Sgt	Dodwell	Wounded in Action	23.2.17
83911	Dr	Baker A.	- do -	25.2.17
L/45189	Gr	Henour A.	- do -	16.2.17
155242	Dr	Preston J.	- do -	12.2.17
10609	Dr	Pinner W.	- do -	24.1.17

70192	Pt	Hodgson L	Wounded Accidentally Died in London Hosptl.	24-3-18
43651	Do	Carvell T.	Killed in Action	24-4-18
24065	Do	Higgins N	Wounded in Action	24-4-18
70527	"	Stewart R	- do -	do
20058	"	Rogers G	- do -	do
18940	Sdlr	Beaver H.	- do -	8-4-18
70244	Do	Hitchin WE	Died Lobar Pneumonia	18-6-18
73436	Do	Eaglen G.	Killed in Action	25-4-18
36936	"	Bridges A.	- do -	do
174368	G.	Fearn W	- do -	do
43661	7Bdr	Goodyer C.	Wounded in Action	25-4-18
5015	G.	Clare E.	"	
54003	S/S	Hewson A.W.B.	"	
86580	Do	Imson HA.	"	
70531	.	Wray H	"	
148390	-	Golden WJ	"	
50605	.	Jackson JR	"	
115483	Bdr	Woolger G.	"	
36395	Do	Brown J	"	
26940	"	Gill E	"	
98054	G.	Powell WJ	"	
122463	Do	Bilton S.	"	
54008	-	Ramsey R.	"	
88060	Bdr	Kentish D	"	
30823	Do	Walsby O.	"	
53999	..	Tuckfield A	"	
120699	-	Ward TJ	"	
229078	-	Jackson W	"	
54320	-	Somers H	"	
L/40251	.	Thomas JR	"	
41735	-	Jones W.	"	
148406	.	Walker G	"	
18941	-	Hall CW	"	
204813	-	Blackwell E	"	
36541	-	Davies E	"	
930280	-	Middleton CA	"	
931206	-	Coburn J	"	
192511	-	Hoey W	" died of Wounds	
68120	-	Field S	} 26-4-18 }	

100114	/Bdr	Robbins A.	Wounded in Action 25-4-18
7619	Dr	Lindsay. A	— do —
			Both died from Wounds 26-4-18
735840	Gr	Wildig W.	Killed in Action 8-11-18
111489	Dr	Foster G.	Died from Pneumonia 3-11-18. Whilst on leave in U.K.
144382	Gr	Holland W.E.	Died from Broncho Pneumonia 6-2-18
83663	Dr	Ralph. R.H.	— do — do -13-12-18
L/26654	—	Smith R.A	— do — do 26-12-18

I joined the 30th Divl. Train at CROWDALL on the 11-12-'14 - from B.E.F. FRANCE, for duty in connection with its formation.

I learnt that the Train had started its formation in Aldershot in Oct. '14 and had moved to CROWDALL in the following month (Nov?)

The Senior Officers at this time were:-
Major E.N.W. Scott Commdg Off.
Capt. N.L. CRAIG S.S.O
T/Capt. F.B. Hardy Adjt.
T/Capt. N.B. Clegg O.C. 158 Co.
T/Lieut W.H. Napper " 159 Co
(R)2/Lt N.R. Hathaway " 160 Co
T/Lieut E.A.K. Meade " 161 Co

The strength of the Train at
this period was approximately:-
   13 Officers
   300 Other ranks
 90 ~~100~~ Riding Horses
   40 H.D.

There were a number of
civilian vehicles of various
patterns on charge, and
at about this time the first
G.S. wagons were received - 6
Mark X vehicles being drawn
from F. Stores, Aldershot.

    The 4 Companies although
existing in name, did not
each have a separate
existence; the accounting
for the greater part being
carried out by 158 Co. for the

whole Train. I was instructed
by the O.C. Train to take the
matter in hand. Separate
accounts were then started
for each company, and the
O.C. Co's & Coms' were instructed
as to the proper methods of
accounting separately.
The Pay & Cash a/cs of 158 Co.
which had been open for the
whole train since its formation
were consequently closed & new
ones opened.
     Up to this period
the NCOs & men had been
well exercised in dismounted
drill, and a limited amount
of instruction in Riding &
wagon drill had been

given. From time to time further small increases were made in the Nom: of Off'rs other ranks, & horses.

Toward the middle of ~~February~~ January 45, Capt: N.L. CRAIG & 4 Officers proceeded to BLACKDOWN, where the Division was quartered, and commenced the duties of feeding the division.

On the 5° Feb: Capt. F.J. Hardy was promoted to T/Major, T/Lieut: W.H. Lapper T/Capt: & Sergt N.R. Hattaway to T/Lieut:,

T/Major F.J. Hardy took command of 158 Co:, I took up appointment of Adj't.

About this time Lieut: W.H. Cadbury

Browne took command of
161 Co: from Lieut. E.A.K Meade,
who took up Supply duties.
The following drills, exercises,
&c were now being proceeded
with:-

    Lectures by O.C. Train.
    Foot drill.
    Riding drill
    Wagon drill
    Harness instruction
    Mounting & dismounting wagons
    Rifle & musketry exercises
    Semaphore signalling

about this time Division moved to WITLEY
About the 3rd week in
February Major E.W.W SCOTT
received orders to proceed
EAST, and was relieved by
Major J.A. HAMILTON who was

on leave to 28th Feb:
Train marched out of CROWDALL to STRATH-FIELD SAYE (Duke of Wellington's estate) on 1st March 1915.
About this time T/Capt N.B. CLEGG proceeded to WITLEY on Supply duties.
All civilian wagons handed in to Field Stores A'Shot.
From time to time further vehicles & equipt were drawn.
Drills and exercises continued daily as heretofore.
Large draft of Supply details arrived from A'Shot & posted to Supply duties at WITLEY.
Train marched out of S'F'DSAYE and entrained at MORTIMER ST. (near READING)

for SALISBURY PLAIN April 13", & on arrival encamped at ROLLESTON CAMP. Division already at LARKHILL, SALISBURY PLAIN

Training continued as usual. Large numbers of remounts received

Further consignment of wagons, harness, arms, & accoutrements, received.

Train commenced feeding division with our own transport. About the end of April 1915 Lieut: Col: C. CONWAY-GORDON arrived and took command of Train. Major S.O. HAMILTON remained. Early in June '15 Lt Col: C. Conway-Gordon left Train with a view to taking up a new appointment. Major J.A. HAMILTON re-assumed command. About middle of June L'Col: C. CONWAY-GORDON returned to Train & re-assumed command. Major J.A. HAMILTON remained. Captain A. DIXON-BROWN had, just before this, taken over command of 16 Co: from Lieut. N.R. HATHAWAY.

Train inspected, as far as possible in full marching order, by Brig. Gen: LANDON, Insp: of A.S.C.

Train transport now fully employed daily on Supply duties, local transport work, and wagon drills.

Division including Train reviewed
+ inspected by H.M. The KING
early in July.
All wagons now complete
and marked.
Horses completed to strength
~~km~~ Full compliment of new
Harness P.D, G.S (American
manufacture) received + all
old harness returned to A.O.D.
All equipment required
to complete as at A.F. G.1097
now drawn.
Company accounts balanced
+ closed. All Home service documents
books + correspondence
disposed of.
Details posted to Field
Ambulance

W.O. N.C.O. & men unfit for
Service disposed of.
"Details to be left at the BASE"
detailed to remain behind with
T/Lieut K.S. MEAGHER.
S.S.O. & certain Supply Officers
proceeded overseas.
Train proceeded over Sea in
the following order ~~the~~ embarking
at ~~HAVRE~~ SOUTHAMPTON and disembarking
at HAVRE :-

Head Qrs. Train } Entrained AMESBURY
158 Co: } 20.7.15.
159 Co:

160 Co.   Entrained AMESBURY
                    20.7.15

161 Co.   Entrained AMESBURY
                    22.7.15

Division including Train concentrated at LUMBRES and vicinity, and marched to MERRIS 28.7.15.

  Head Qrs Train MERRIS
  & 158 Co
  159 Co: VIEUX BERQUIN
  160 Co OOTERSTEENE
  161 Co:
CAPT. DIXON-BROWN proceeded to ENGLAND &
LIEUT. HATHAWAY took command 160 Co
    Whole of Train
Marched to ESTAIRES 28.8.15
@ LOOS offensive 25.9.15.

T/Major F.B. HARDY proceeded to ENGLAND for duty and T/Capt W. Cadbury-Browne took Command 158 Co:
T/Capt G.H.A. LOWE took Command of 161 Co:

HISTORY OF No 1 SECTION 20th D.A.C.

No 1 SECTION 20th D.A.C was formed on 15-1-1915 and went into training. It left England with the other Sections from LARKHILL SALISBURY PLAIN for France on the 22nd July 1915 arriving at HAVRE on the morning of the 24th July 1915, departed same day for LUMBRES arriving at 6-30 am on the 26th July 1915 and marched from there to AFFRINGUES on 27th, left AFFRINGUES for ARQUES on 28th, left ARQUES 29th for SOUVERAIN and remained there until 2nd August 1915 when the 18pr and S.A.A. Sub-Sections of the Section proceeded to SENECHAL to be attached for duty with the 8th Divisional Ammunition Column, & remained with them until 30th August 1915 during which period it was assisting 8th Div in supplying Ammunition both to their Infantry & to their guns.

Section rejoined 20th DAC to a billet just outside ESTAIRES on the NEUF BERQUIN-ESTAIRES ROAD and remained there until 21st Sept 1915 and owing to forthcoming operations an Ammunition dump called the PARK DUMP was established at the Sections Camp under the command of Capt. L.A.W. BROOKS R.F.A. who was O.C of this Section, throughout the whole of this month great progress was made in the erection of Stables & Shelters etc for the Animals of the Section, during the month the

Stables were visited and inspected by the D.A & Q.M.G 3rd Corps who was satisfied with the progress made, On the 23rd November 1915 the G.O.C R.A. 20th Div inspected the Section in full marching order - and he considered the turn out very satisfactory. On 30th November 1915 the D.D.R inspected the Horses of the Section and expressed great satisfaction as to their condition.

On Decr 3rd 1915 Capt L.A.W. BROOKS RFA reported sick and was sent to Hospital leaving 2/Lieut. C.H.M Pearson R.F.A in temporary command of the Section. On the 6th Decr 1915 Lieut. A.T. Gulliver arrived from the 93rd Bde R.F.A. and assumed the temporary command of the Section, 2/Lieut R.E. Rawson R.F.A. who was a Subaltern in the Section was sent to 93rd Bde RFA for attachment. Lieut. T.A. Codner R.F.A having arrived from the 93rd Bde RFA on the 13th is posted to the Command of No 1 Section 20th D.A.C. Capt. L.A.W. Brooks RFA invalided to England on 15th Decr and struck off the strength. 2/Lieut W.W. RICHARDS. RFA transferred from No 3 Section to No 1 Section & 2/Lieut. C.H.M. PEARSON from No 1 Section to No 3 on 1st January 1916 Lieut. A.T. Gulliver posted to No 1 Section on 12th January 1916.

On the 22nd January 1916 the Section marched out with the remainder of the Column to join the rest of the Division to join the II Army, arrived LETIR ANGLAIS HAZEBROUCK & bivouaced for the night. The Section Column consisting of Hd Qrs Nos 1, 2 & 3 Sections continued their march arriving at LEDERZEELE at about 4pm on 23rd Jany 1916 On the 31st Jany the D.D.R 2nd Army inspected the Horses and found them to his entire satisfaction. On the 4th Feby the Section moved from LEDERZEELE to ARNEKE, advance parties were sent under the command of Lieut. A. J. GULLIVER RFA to the POPERHINGE area to take over the camp lately occupied by No 1 Section of the 14th D.A.C. The Section moved from ARNEKE to the POPERHINGE area on the 14th in the early hours of the morning. The Section took up position at A.18.c.6.2. (Sheet 28) as an advanced Section, supplying the whole of the Ammunition requirements of the Division, Wagons from Brigade Ammunition Columns fetching the Ammunition to the dump, Lieut R.G. Russell RFA attached to the Section for duty on 13th March 1916. By order of the Second Army the Wagons of the Section were reduced to 28, The surplus wagons being sent to the 1st & 2nd Canadian Divisions

Lieut R.G. Russell transferred from Section to 93rd Bde R.F.A. on March 18th. No 70094 Bombr. G. Plunkett died of wounds received in action on 26th March whilst attached to right group Artillery. Section continued in the supply of the whole of the Ammunition to the Division.

On the 19th April 1916 the Section with other Sections and Hd Qrs moved off to the Reserve Area & arrived at BOLLEZEELE & owing to the Units of the 6th Division not having moved out of the billets at RUBROUCK the Section was compelled to bivouac the night at BOLLEZEELE. Officers & men of the 6th DAC arrived at Section to take over Ammunition and Camp Stores prior to our moving to the reserve Area. Section remained in this Area for rest of the month during which period Lectures on various subjects for Officers were given at D.A.C. Hd Qrs. Whilst in the line 20 HCs Then were lent to the Brigades for the purpose of preparing advanced positions.

The L.D & H.D Horses were gradually taken from the Section by orders of the D.D.R 2nd Army & replaced by mules.

On the 12th May arrangements were made to reorganise the Column owing to the absorption

2 Brigade Ammn Columns in the D.A.C, all Surplus Officers, NCO & men, also Animals, Harness and carts to go to the Base Calais when the reorganisation is completed. The Column was reformed into 4 Sections, Capt Wright to Command No 1 Section 20th D.A.C. & Capt. T.A Codnor to Command No 2 Section. The details surplus left by road under the Command of Lieut Richards for the Base Calais. After having sent the advance parties early on the morning of the 19th inst to PESEL HOEK to take over from the Guards D.A.C the Section left the RUBROUCK area at 5 am with the remaining Sections under the Command of LIEUT-COL .J.R. FOSTER. R.F.a, and proceeded to PESEL HOEK arriving there at about 1-30 pm being responsible for the Ammunition Supply for the Division from 6 pm on 20th May, It was arranged to work the Ammunition Supply from a central dump at D.A.C. Hd Qrs issues being to the Section & the Section delivering to Battery Gun positions & Infantry Brigade Transport lines, On 23rd inst the

CORPS COMMANDER (LIEUT-GEN LORD CAVAN)- visited the Section accompanied by the 14th Corps DAA & Q.M.G (Brig Gen Cooke).

On the 30th May Capt Wright R.F.A Commanding the Section was appointed Assistant Instr in Equitation to Second Army & left the Unit on the 31st inst to take up this appointment Lieut. W.T. HILL, RFA of No 2 Section being appointed in temporary Command of the Section. On June 1st 1916 the Section received orders to take up a new position at VLAMERTINGHE & proceeded there on that date. On 3rd June Capt A.E. WRIGHT was appointed Asst Instr of Equitation 2nd Army, CAPT. F.C ROSS-BROWN to Command the Section.

On 5th June 1916 the Section lines came under very heavy shell fire with the result that 5 horses were killed. Shelling was very severe in and around the lines & on the 8th June sanction was obtained to move the lines a quarter of a mile South of VLAMERTINGHE leaving the Ammunition dump on the VLAMERTINGE Road which was a good & handy site for a dump. On June 18th CAPT. F.C. ROSS-BROWN was appointed Adjutant of the 90th Bde RFA and CAPT. H.P. BERESFORD-PEER to Command No 1 Section. The Ammunition requirements of the Batteries during the month were very heavy and owing to this and the absence of men from the Section to replace Casualties in the Batteries & for work on O.Ps the Section was kept at very high pressure for the whole of this period, & continued until 8/9/16 when the Section together with remainder of DAC marched to CARNOY arriving there on 14/9/16 Before marching to CARNOY Lieut. S.R. REYNOLDS was posted to the Section. On arrival at CARNOY the Section was attached to the 24th D.A.C. and supplied Ammunition to the 91st Bde RFA which was in action North of COMBLES, on 29th inst Section came under the orders of 20th DAC Hd Qrs who took over responsibility for Ammn supply from that day. Ammunition was being delivered to Battery positions by the Section up to 4/10/16 when all roads & tracks were in such a state that it was impossible to carry on with this system of delivery any longer as wagons got stuck in the mud although 8 & 10 horses were tried but to no effect in consequence of which pack animals had to be used which turned out to be a very successful experiment & the Ammunition was being delivered to Batteries up to 11th inst when the first issue by train was made to GUILLEMONT Station & thence from there to Batty positions by pack. On 16th inst work was commenced on dump at MARICOURT Stone Siding which when completed, the G.S. Wagons Carted Ammunition from there to a forward dump on the BRIEQETRIE Road & Batteries collected from this forward dump & from there it would be taken by them to their respective Batteries.

On the 26th November 1916 all Ammunition dumps was handed over to 2nd Australian Div & all fatigues for XIVth Corps ceased on this date. The Section together with R.A.H.Q. & 91st Bde RFA left their camp and proceeded to rest area, halting at CORBIE for the night & remained at MORLANCOURT until the 27th December 1916 after spending a good month there.

Section arrived at CARNOY and took over Camp occupied by No. 3 Section, commencing next day in erecting a suitable standing Camp both for Men and Animals, Reorganisation of the R.A Commences on 13th January 1917, Consequent upon Reorganisation the establishments of A Echelon is increased and that of Echelon "B" slightly diminished, Deficiencies in Echelon "A" are made up from No 3 Section who were being turned into an Army Field Artillery Brigade Column, all Small Arms were handed over to No 4 Section who were being turned into a S.A.A Section only. Work was carried on during the rest of the month in Completing Camp, occasionally assisting Batteries with Pack animals for their Ammunition supply and a few wagons and teams for drawing Gun line material, and the same during the month of February 1917. Lieut P.W. Hamilton joined No 1 Section from No 3 Section on reorganisation of D.A.C on 13th January 1917.

On 1st March Section took charge of GUILLEMONT Ammunition dump from 17th Divl Artillery and Lieut Wyer then belonging to the Section was appointed to Command this dump.

An ammunition dump was also formed at COMBLES on 19th March when enemy Commenced to retire, The Section then moved forward to LEUZE WOOD and there was camped, The Animals were camped on shell torn Country, the weather being very bad with the result that they were Standing in a foot of mud after a few days, numerous cases of cracked and greasy heels the Animals suffered from and it became very hard to keep up the condition of them, As the enemy retired, So forward dumps were established, The 1st at BUS on the Southern edge where Ammunition was within 200 yards of the Battery positions, The Section was employed in Carting Ammunition from COMBLES dump (which was the rear dump) to the forward dump at BUS, occasionally coming under shell fire, on one occasion Lieut. H. Maynard had arrived with 24 wagons of Ammn for the dump, & apparently was seen by the enemy who were then at a village named YTRES a matter of 1½ miles from BUS because they opened fire on his convoy with a Battery of light Field Guns, fortunately they misjudged the range which gave Lieut Maynard a chance to remove his teams to a place of safety & thereby saving casualties, The Ammunition was then ordered by him to be carried by the Gunners in their packs to the dump, a walk of about 300 yards. On the 25th March the Divl Ammn Column was transferred from XIVth Corps to the XVth, during the whole month dumps were being refilled in the forward area at the same time special efforts were made and a systematic clearance was effected from the forward area & vacated Battery positions of all kinds of Ammunition & empties, this work continued until the 17th April when the Section moved forward to BUS and selected a wagon line in an orchard on the northern edge of the village. No billets were available for the men as the village had been destroyed by the enemy before his departure, so tents & shelters were erected in and around the camp, the whole being well screened from the enemy by tall trees. The enemy were then retiring gradually on St QUENTIN. The Ammunition dump was moved from BUS to NEUVILLE-BOURJONVAL which was taken charge of by Lieut. W.W. WYER. During the latter part of this month the COMBLES dump was gradually cleared & the ammunition brought forward to BUS dump, which the Section assisted in.

On 1st May 1917 ammunition was delivered by the Section to advanced positions of the 92nd Bde RFA on the Southern outskirts of METZ-en-COUTURE which was receiving special attention by the enemy, luckily no casualties and returned to camp at about 3 a.m on 2nd inst. This procedure was again carried out in the evening of the 2nd, as teams would be under close observation if taken up during the day. On the 3rd inst 10 G.S Wagons under the command of Lieut. R.S Hamilton was detailed to draw 300 boxes of boxed Ammunition from railhead ROCQUIGNY & delivered to dump at NEUVILLE which was carried out with one casualty to a Horse from Shell fire. On the 4th & 5th inst all G.S Wagons turned out twice to collect boxed Ammunition from this Railhead for delivery to dump at NEUVILLE. On the 7th

May, after the enemy had further retired. Lorries carried 4000 Rds of Shrapnel 18pr to NEUVILLE dump thereby greatly assisting the Section who were then being very heavily worked. On the 8th the Section collected 350 Rounds of 4-5 How Ammunition from a vacated Battery position and carted it to their new position, North of METZ-en-COUTURE. On 14th inst G.O.C. Division inspected Section Camp & expressed himself quite satisfied. On the 14th at 9pm 5 Wagons & teams proceeded to QUEENS CROSS 2 miles N of METZ en COUTORE with Ammunition. On this occasion the teams had a very lucky escape. On returning through METZ-en-COUTURE, The enemy opened out a terrific rate of fire on the village which necessitated the teams turning back & returning by another route. On 18th all wagons filled up their echelons of Ammunition from BUS and NEUVILLE in preparation for expected relief and move. All boxed Ammunition was carted forward to a dump at VAULX. On 30th Section moved forward to a wagon line 1 mile due

N of Bapaume. On 3rd June Pit props and Camouflaged gun covers were drawn from R.E dumps and delivered to Battery positions, also for next few days all empty cartridge cases were salved from the Battery positions. On 11th June 1000 Rds of Ammunition was delivered to D/91 RFA and each day onwards great assistance was given to 91st Bde RFA in delivering Ammunition to their gun positions. Section moved to rest area at MAMETZ on relief of 62nd Divl Artillery. The latter part of the month was spent in making up deficiencies & replacing unserviceable articles also by painting & overhauling all vehicles. On 3rd July Section moved with remainder of Column en route for YPRES Salient arriving at PESELHOEK and arrived there on 12th. Work was commenced in anticipation of the Battle of PILKHEM ridge & 10 wagon loads of Ammunition was loaded from 38th Divl dump & delivered to Batteries which were in position near BOESINGHE 5 Animals were wounded through Shell fire in approaching Battery positions, all Ammunition delivered. 14th July the Section delivered 10 G.S wagon loads of Ammunition to Battery positions

15th 15 GS Wagon loads of Ammn to Battery positions
16th 14   =   =   =   =   =
17th 15   =   =   =   =   =

On the 17th the Sections Convoy was in charge of Lt. F.W. Wyles & when returning to camp after delivery of Ammunition via DAWSONS CORNER & ELVERDINGHE the whole party came under very heavy fire Lieut Wyles was very badly wounded, Sergt White then took charge of the party, collected them & galloped through the barrage losing 3 Horses killed and 2 wounded, He got the pieces off to Clearing Station & was responsible for a good piece of work in having so few casualties.
18th & 19th saw us delivering Ammunition as fast as we could get backwards & forwards, At each journey suffering casualties to both Men & Animals & all ranks admitted that it was the worse battle they had been in.
On 20th inst Lieut P.W. Hamilton with a party of 25 Wagons & teams left Camp at 6-30pm en route for Battery positions via Elverdinghe & came under very heavy shell fire, chiefly liquid fire & gas. This Officer ordered his teams out of the village as it appeared madness

to venture right through the village, All Men & teams were got safely away with the exception of one team which fortunately had a very narrow escape, A shell burst about 5 yards from this particular team blowing the 3 drivers off their Horses, The animals took fright & ran into the ditch breaking the pole, The Officer & Sergt White replaced the pole from the spare one carried under the wagon & got the team away with the others. Another route was decided upon by the Officer with the result that the Convoy proceeded via HOSPITAL CORNER, DAWSONS CORNER ESSEX FARM & CHEAPSIDE, At Cheapside the Convoy was once more unfortunate meeting with gas Shells, The Officer immediately ordered Gas masks on and managed with great difficulty in getting to the Battery positions which was then about 4am on 2/prist. The teams were returned independantly so as not to have a congestion of traffic on the road, which was for the best as just as the last two teams were being unloaded another Section arrived on the Battery position just when the enemy opened out their fire resulting in very bad casualties to both Men & Horses. On 22nd the Section Convoy under Lieut. N. Tweedale whilst proceeding to Battery positions a building and dump were blown up and in passing this spot a portion of the Convoy was observed & heavily shelled, Severe Casualties in killed & wounded other ranks & animals were sustained from shell fire & gas shells and it was found impossible owing to the road being blocked by dead animals, smashed vehicles etc to deliver part of the ammunition. On 23rd by means of fatigue parties, fresh teams & drivers under Command of Capt H.P.B. Poer & 2nd Lt Hamilton the undelivered ammunition was delivered and wagons & pieces of wagons brought back to the Section. On the same night a convoy was again sent forward to Battery positions, this time in charge of Lieut. H. MAYNARD who had a very adventurous journey, having to move dead animals & broken vehicles off the road leading into ELVERDINGHE, but he managed to arrive at positions intact & complete his job. On 24th 1000 Rds of gas shells were taken to Battery positions. This state of affairs went on until the enemy had been driven back to PASSCHENDALE. Section moved to Camp 200yds of ELVERDINGHE, during the latter half of the month the Section was called upon to work very hard & during the period 19th to 26th (one week) 12,000 rounds of ammunition was delivered to Battery positions in addition to returning & sending up water to Batteries, also quantities of constructional material & camouflage were supplied and guns brought out & taken into action as the wagon lines of Batteries were 10 miles in rear so as to keep them fresh in the event of a break through. For this work all Sections was congratulated by the CRA. 20th Div. during the month of August work was chiefly carried out in carting ammunition to Batteries from their old positions to their positions they advanced to and in salving empty cartridge cases, in addition to which daily supplies of ammunition was transported from a dump on ELVERDINGE Rd to a dump known as BARDS on the CANAL BANK BARDS CAUSEWAY. It was forgotten to mention for acts of courage & gallantry displayed on 14th & 20th July Sergt White was recommended by Lieut R. Hamilton on account of Coolness displayed & the great assistance that he was to this Officer for which this N.C.O received the Military Medal. During the month of September Intensive Salvage work was carried out in Clearing all tracks & Gun positions in addition daily Convoys were found for Supplying forward dump with Ammunition from Rear dumps on the 11th inst the Convoy came under a Bomb attack during the day whilst in Charge of Lieut H Maynard resulting in 2 men killed, one wounded and 1 Horse Killed & 3 wounded. On 12th Several bombs were dropped in vicinity of Camp which necessitated moving the Animals from the lines, Capt H.P.B. POER R.F.A who was Commanding the Section displayed great coolness in Arranging for removal of Camp & gave great assistance to helping a Section of the Guards D.A.C who came under very heavy fire in removing & attending the wounded, A number of pack animals was employed in carting Ammunition to prepared Battery positions on the STEENBECQ river also under cover of darkness material was carried by the Sections wagons to the same prepared positions. Sergt Burrell who was NCO I/c of one of these parties came under heavy fire on one occasion in which he showed great coolness & although it appeared an impossible journey owing to enemy shell fire he managed with great difficulty in getting his 3 wagons to their destination getting one blown up on his return journey, but no casualties to men or Horses. On another occasion Sergt. A. Cundy who was NCO with Lieut P.W. Hamilton delivering Ammun to positions on the STEENBECQ gave valuable assistance when teams came under Shell fire & on various occasions when he had Sole Charge of parties his work was carried out with disregard to his own personal safety & at all times this NCO never failed in delivering his Ammunition to the Batteries thereby setting a splendid example to the men. For the good work done by this

NOTE that P.W. HAMILTON was specially mentioned in despatches for work & devotion to duty during YPRES Campaign of Co the D.C.M was awarded him early in 1918. During the latter part of ~~October~~ Sept. quantities of Ammunition was taken up to Battery positions both by wagons & packs for use in the operations opened out N.E of LANGEMARCK. From 1st to 18th October assistance was given to Batteries on the STEENBECQ RIVER both with Ammunition Supply and Carting of Gun line material. Casualties to men & Animals were very small during this period. On the 20th inst the Section entrained at PROVEN (at the same time thankful to be relieved after a most trying time to all ranks) for PERONNE and from thence to NURLU by road pending relief of 40th D.A.C. The latter part of this month was spent in supplying numerous wagons for Infantry & R.E's. On 1st Nov. to 14th parties were found for dump for unloading Decauville trains with Ammunition from 14th to 20th Ammunition was drawn from Railhead & delivered to Sections Camp for refilling Batteries & Section. A forward dump was formed on GOUZECOURT— LA VACQUERIE Road in charge of Lieut. H. Maynard, after enemy had been forced out of the HINDENBURG LINE. On 22nd 2 teams proceeded to QUENNÉT FARM to bring in two captured German guns, from 23rd onwards to end of month Salvage was carried out, On 21st November Lieut Maynard with dump party was captured by the enemy at his dump near GOUZEAUCOURT, Bor Sample & Gnr Watkins who were 2 of his party succeeded in escaping after hiding in a Shell hole for 7 hours. The Section onwards from this date carried out the usual Ammunition supply to Batteries & various Salvage jobs after which on 15th December it marched to ROBECQ arriving there on 24th December & resting there until 29th inst when it moved with remainder of Column to CROIX de POPERHINGHE, Capt H. P. B. POER R.F.A was posted to A/91 R.F.A on promotion to Major. Lieut P.W. HAMILTON being appointed acting CAPTAIN to command NO 1 SECTION Arriving at destination 31st inst. remaining in this rest area until 21st January 1918 during which period wagons were overhauled & repairs carried out to harness etc, On 21st Jany Section marched out to a Camp close to ZEVECOTEN relieving the 34th Divl Artillery and remained in this Camp until 14th Feby 1918 during which period Road work & material carted was carried out. The Section marched out to CROIX-de POPERHINGE on 17th inst & remained there until 19th inst when it marched out en route to MORBECQUE area, arriving there on 20th inst. On 23rd The Section entrained at STEENBECQUE & detrained at NESLE from thence by road to OFFOY & there remained refitting etc until 21st March when the Section suddenly got orders at 2-30pm to at once take up a Wagon line at SAINT-SIMON a Camp evacuated by the 36th DAC in the morning. On arrival in this village it was noticed that it was receiving attention from the enemy who was sending over 6" air bursts over the Camp & Water troughs. It was decided to get men & animals under cover at once and Capt Hamilton reported to Staff Capt 36th Div to whom Section was attached to for duty, during the period of waiting for the reply 1 Horse was killed and 3 wounded. Orders were received at 9pm to at once proceed to AUBIGNY & select a wagon line on the AUBIGNY-HAM road and about 500 yards from the village, as the enemy were advancing on St-SIMON. The Section arrived at about 11-30pm being held up by numerous Columns etc & awaited orders. As no orders were received by 3pm on 22nd inst And that it was noticed that all Guns & wagons were retiring It was decided to retire on HAM being the last Wheeled Unit to move, Guides was at once sent out to reconnoitre the Battery of the 36th Div to whom this Section was supposed to supply Ammunition to. Lieut Gibbard discovered that they were retiring on OFFOY - CANAL BANK to which place the Section proceeded to, The Gun line being found, Capt Hamilton reported to Lieut-Col Sotter DSO who was Commanding a Group of Artillery in the 36th Div who informed him that he was retiring to BLACENCOORT on the HAM-NESLE Road And that I had to select wagon lines at BREUILLE a village 1½ miles in rear, And that his Batteries were very low in Ammunition. The Section completed their establishments of Ammunition & refilled at GUYANCOURT at the same time loading all wagons with 4 boxes more than their establishment in case Ammunition wasn't available, the following morning Batteries were ordered to retire on ESMERY HALLON to which place the Section retired to picking up on the way 200 4-5 Charges, On arrival

Orders were received that the Batteries would take up positions on CANAL BANK FRESNIES in consequence the Section supplied Batteries with Ammunition & took up & Wagon line 1 mile in rear at which Camp the enemy machine gunned the Camp from Aircraft resulting in 3 Horses being wounded and one killed. All ranks collected their rifles & fired at planes who were very low. At this place the Section managed to get into touch with Staff Capt. 36th Div who ordered O.C to report to 36th D.A.C. who were then camped at AVRICOORT & from then onwards to 8th April the Section assisted this DAC in supplying Ammunition to Batteries, filling up dumps, Supplying Rations and forage to Batteries. At this time the men and animals were practically done, marching & returning to Batteries with Ammunition & then retiring from 21st March to 8th April, practically 40 miles a day was done. Then orders were received to report with Section at SENARPONT and join remainder of 20th D.A.C at which place Section arrived on 9th April. Horses were watered & fed & men turned out to dinner & a good sleep which every man had earnt. On the 10th April Orders were suddenly received to join 91st Bde RFA at VILLERS-BRETTONEUX via. VERS and arrived at destination on the 12th reported to LIEUT-COL- A.E. ERSKINE DSO who was Commanding Bde whose headquarters advanced were at the CHATEAU near VILLERS-BRETTONEUX. The Section being camped at ~~VILLERS-BRETTONEUX~~ BLANGY TRONVILLE. A dump was established near this village and ammunition supplied to Batteries up to 21st when remainder of DAC arrived from whom all orders regarding supply of ammunition to Batteries were received from. On 23rd a convoy of Section was approaching the gun positions when it came under very heavy shell and machine gun fire, the enemy having advanced to the ridge a few hundred yards from Batty positions resulting in the following casualties, 1 man killed & 3 wounded. On this occasion

All Battery Commanders & the O.C. 91st Bde highly praised Capt Hamilton for the gallantry displayed by all ranks on that eventful morning and that there was no individual case that could be brought forward for recognition as all ranks were worthy. On 24th Another day of heavy shelling resulting in a few more casualties and on this occasion Capt Hamilton recommended two drivers. Dr. Marson & Dr Quigley for awards for the following acts of gallantry, Dr Marsons lead driver with his horses were wounded at were being heavily shelled. The Centre driver Dr Quigley & the wheel Driver Dr Marson extricated wounded animals, Dr Quigley carrying the wounded man to the Hospital at a distance of 3 miles and Dr Marson with his two wheel Horses proceeding at once to the Battery gun positions (who where then very short of ammunition) & delivered all his ammunition, for this act of gallantry

Dr Mason was awarded the Military Medal & Dr Quigley mentioned in despatches. On 25th the wagon line was being so heavily shelled that orders were received from Hd Qrs to move back to a wood near CAMON remaining there until 28th during which period Ammunition was supplied to Batteries. For these operations SERGT BURRELL was recommended for valuable assistance & devotion to duty for which he was awarded the M.S.M. On 28th Section moved back to SALOUEL (South west of AMIENS) and on the 30th Section with remainder of DAC marched to GOUY-SERVINS on transfer of 25th Divl Arty from fourth to first Army arriving there on 4th May 1918 relieving the 3rd Canadian DAC. At this place the Section remained until October 7th 1918. Work was chiefly carried out in carting material for R.E's Road repairs, no Ammunition was delivered owing to the Decauville railways proving themselves so capable in keeping Batteries up to establishments, they taking it direct to their gun positions. On 25th July at about 11-30pm severe casualties were sustained in the Section Camp by a severe attack by Hostile Aircraft, 7 Bombs being dropped in the Camp resulting in 7 Men being killed and 34 wounded, great assistance being given by Captain Swift M.C. R.A.M.C & the Officers of the Section in attending to the wounded which was a very trying time owing to numerous enemy planes being over the Camp at the time which necessitated no lights being Shewn. Capt Hamilton was slightly wounded but remained with Unit, 2 Horses were wounded and two of the billets of the Men were practically demolished although mud walls had been built around them to the extent of 3½ feet.

On October 7th the Section marched from GOUY-SERVINS via VILLERS-AU-BOIS and MONT-ST-ELOY to ARRAS. Wagon lines were formed on the ARRAS-AMIENS road - about 1 Kilometre from the town.

The weather was raining and the animals were picketted out in the open - the men being billetted in empty houses.

The Section remained at ARRAS until the 9th when it marched via ARRAS and GUEMAPPE to a wagon line which had been chosen on the CHERISY-VIS-EN-ARTOIS road.

Considerable difficulty was experienced in forming a compact camp & wagon line on account of the extraordinary number of shell holes & craters & the amount of barbed wire & debris laying about.

The Section remained here until the 30th of Oct - during which period - a large number of remounts were collected from ARRAS and delivered to units in the CAMBRAI area.

A good deal of Salvage work was also carried out - voluntarily - and the Section was responsible for the salving of at least £2,000 worth of stores and ammunition of all kinds, which was dumped on the main ARRAS - CAMBRAI road.

On the 30th of October the Section marched via - VIS-EN-ARTOIS - and MARQUION - to CAMBRAI and billetted in the MARWITZ BARRACKS in that town.

This move was consequent upon Transfer of the Divisional artillery to the 3rd ARMY.

From the 30th of October till Nov. 2nd the Section remained in CAMBRAI, during which period was fully occupied by cleaning up of wagons and harness.

On the 2nd of Nov. the Section received orders to march via NAYES to the vicinity of SAULZOIR where wagon lines were formed on the SAULZOIR - MONTRÉCOURT road. The march was carried out under most trying conditions - the roads being in a bad state of repair & the weather very wet & cold. On the same afternoon a reconnaissance was carried out with the object of siting a wagon line in the vicinity of VENDEGIES.

On the 3rd November the Section marched to the wagon lines selected on the previous afternoon

and bivouacked on the VERCHAIN
VENDEGIES-road.
This march was carried out in the
early hours of the morning — arriving
at the Wagon lines about 9am.
Ammunition was at once sent up
to the Btys in the neighbourhood of
MARESCHES.
This was accomplished under intense
shellfire of the Enemy who had
the whole road under observation.
The column succeeded in
delivering the ammunition and
returned to Camp with one or
two minor casualties.
The Section remained in this Camp
until the 6th of November.
During this period — rain fell
incessantly turning the wagon
lines into a veritable quagmire.
Horses were standing almost
up to their hocks in mud, the

Officers + NCO's then being
bivouaked in the open.
On the 6th of November - orders were
received to march to wagon
lines in the VILLERS-POL - area
in order to facilitate supply of
ammunition to the Batteries, which
was becoming a very difficult
task on account of the rapidity
of the advance.
O/c No 1 Section Capt. P.W. Hamilton,
had to ride forward daily
sometimes twice daily in order
to locate the Batteries.
Ammunition was taken forward
and dumped in rear of the
Batteries: the Batteries sending
back to these dumps when they
required replenishment of ammn.
Owing to the nature of the
roads - rapidity of advance -
and inclement weather

"The ammunition lorries could only just keep touch."

On Nov. 7th Section marched to and billetted in WARGNIES-LE-GRAND, and remained there the night after having delivered ammunition to the 21st B'de.

On Nov. 8th Section marched and billetted at PLAT-DE-BOIS - west of ST. WAAST - on the main VALENCIENNES MAUBEUGE-road.

Up to this time the column had pushed forward daily - maintaining close touch with the Batteries - thus ensuring prompt and systematic supply of ammunition. Dumps and Battery positions in rear were cleared as the Section moved forward.

On Nov. 11th orders were received from 20th D.A. Arty. H.Q. to the effect that column would remain in billets until further orders.

The period 11th — 22nd Nov. was occupied by refitting and repair and cleaning of wagons etc.

On the 22nd Nov. the Section marched and billetted in POMMIER — (via CAMBRAI — BAPAUME — and HANNESCAMPS) — where it formed permanent billets and stables and demobilized.

No 9.

20 Div. D.A.C.

20 Bn. M.G.C.

Trench Mortars

A.V.C.

20. Div. Train

History of No 2 Section 20th Divl Ammn Column R.F.A.

This Section was prior to the reorganization of the B.A.C.s and D.A.C in May 1916 known as No 1 Section and was commanded by Captain L.A.W. BROOKS. R.F.A. on its arrival in France. It was first formed in March 1915 at Milford, Witley Camp but most of the personnel had joined the Division at Deepcut in the latter days of 1914 and the early days of 1915. Its training for the first few months was chiefly composed of Marching and Setting Up Drill with an occasional route march and, not until the latter days of May 1915 when some Horses were posted, was it possible to start training the Drivers in Riding & Horsemastership at Rollestone Camp, Salisbury Plain. Even then there were many difficulties to be faced because there was no proper Harness or Equipment available and the little that was done was made possible with civilian gear that had been given for the purpose. In the latter days of June Harness & Equipment was issued and from that time onward real useful work went on until the Section embarked for France on the 23rd of July 1915 made up with raw and untrained Mules which had only been drawn from the Remount Depôt a few weeks before.

On its arrival in France the Drivers & Animals were practically of an unknown quantity having had very little training. It is not necessary to stretch one's imagination very far to realize what a difficult and wonderful performance it was to get the Section entrained at Amesbury and detrained & embarked at Southampton & disembarked at Le Havre and finally entrained for its destination to take up its duties as a working Unit in the Line. It started serious work at Neuf Berquin in August 1915 and fed the Brigade Columns whose Batteries came into action between FLEURBAIX & Laventie. After the operations on the 25th Sept 1915 orders were issued to start building Stabling. This was a difficult job to tackle with improvised material and through lack of experience proved a failure. Consequently the mud was terrible. In December 1915 Captain L.A.W. Brooks through illness returned to England and Captain T.A. Codner R.F.A was posted from D/93 Bde R.F.A to command the Section. It was then decided to make another attempt to build stables and the job was tackled by all ranks in earnest it being quite impossible to carry on and face the terrible mud any longer. Within a fortnight a stable to accomodate all the animals, i.e. 250, was erected and the Section was highly complimented by General Hotham and other inspecting Officers on the splendid structure which had been put up and which was spoken of as the best stabling in France. It was admitted that the lines on which this stable was constructed were the most advantageous in every respect and it has since been copied and more or less standardized in all Wagon Lines. In the latter part of January 1916 the Section joined the remainder of the Artillery which came into action on the Brielen front in Feb 1916. The Section started a Dump on the ELVERDINGHE road on the east side of the old windmill. It issued all kinds of Ammunition including Small Arms, French Mortar and Grenades etc. This was the first experiment of running a Dump of a fairly large character well forward & it was considered by some that it was rather risky because all the eggs were in one basket, but the satisfactory working and the greater convenience attached to a Dump of this kind was agreed. It was in May 1916 that the Section became amalgamated with the 9ᵗʰ Bde Ammn Column and it was then known as No 2 Section being made up of approximately 50% of the personnel of each unit. It was then a complete horse Unit with

250 Horses. The Section then worked up into the Ypres area again with the R.A. to PESLEHOEK a Dump being established on the Vlamertinghe Road and supplied half the Divisional Artillery with Ammunition direct to the Batteries every night. During the period the Artillery were in the Ypres Sector in 1916 the Sections of the D.A.C. worked the Ammunition Dump, and supplied by Limbers all the Ammunition direct to the Batteries without any help from the Battery Wagon Lines who were at the rear of Poperinghe. The work was of a very difficult nature practically all of it had to be carried out at night owing to the roads being under observation from the enemy. This fact the enemy was aware of and nearly every night he strafed the roads which he had taped off very accurately. Considering the large amount of Ammunition that was shot off by the Batteries daily this was a very creditable performance entailing a great amount of hard work for all ranks who also had to look after the horses by day. The Section left Ypres Sector during the latter days of September 1916 and marched direct to the Somme with the Divisional Artillery which was inspected by General Plumer en route. It was then attached for Ammunition supply to the 92 Bde R.F.A. which came into action near Guillemont and cooperated with the Batteries in supplying direct to

the guns the enormous amount of Ammunition that was daily expended. All the work was carried out at night and very early morning and it was only with difficulty that the guns could be kept up to establishment. With the advent of the terrible mud Packs were first used it being found impossible to get Wagons up to the Batteries even with 16 Horses hooked in a Wagon. During this terrible and trying period only those who experienced the work can realize what a strain was put upon the N.C.O.s & splendid little Drivers who had to work night & day to keep up the Ammunition supply & keep their Horses in a fit condition. With the exception of about 10 days rest at Morlancourt in January 1917 this Section was continually in action and its Wagon Lines were at Carnoy. It moved up to Combles in February 1917 near Leuze Wood when snow was very thick upon the ground & all ranks lived under canvas, but these conditions were preferable to the mud fields of Carnoy. Eventually the Section came out of action with the remainder of the R.A. in June 1917 and after resting and reequipping at Fricourt it marched with the remainder of the R.A. back to the old battlefield of Ypres. It formed its Wagon Line in Reselhoek Wood on the 12" of July 1917 & started supplying material to make up the new battery positions which were to be occupied by the guns a few days later. The Battery Wagon Lines were on the west side of Poperinghe

6

and the whole of the supply of ammunition for the great preparatory bombardment which lasted about 10 days prior to the 30th of July 1917 fell upon the D.A.C.. In addition to the supply of Ammunition this Section rationed the Batteries of the 92 Bde RFA and also pulled guns out of action as & when they were frequently knocked out & took them back to the I.O.M. in exchange for others. During this period all ranks worked with splendid keenness night & day with scarcely any rest and it certainly achieved one of its best performances during the war. It suffered many casualties and it was only with the greatest difficulty that the enormous expenditure of Ammunition could be met, with the personnel & animals at its disposal. After the 30 July 1917 when the Battle commenced the Batteries advanced & their Wagon Lines came up the supply of Ammunition & material for the new gun positions was carried on continually. It should be mentioned that the Decauville's were blown up so thoroughly by the enemy's shell fire that they were of very little assistance to the Field guns. The Batteries advanced from one position to another until they reached the STEENBECK when the Divisional Artillery was pulled out of action on the 18th Oct 1917. During these terrible 3 months too much praise cannot be given to the splendid little Drivers & their Horses & Mules who kept the guns supplied. On the 21st Oct 1917 the Section entrained with the 92 Bde RFA at Peselhoek siding its destination being Peronne. On arrival it went into Wagon Lines recently vacated by the 40th Divisional Artillery at Nurlu and it was then hoped that a good rest had at last come but this hope was soon knocked on the head & preparations were made for supplying material & Ammunition to new forward battery positions which were to be occupied by the Batteries for the commencement of the Battle of Cambrai. No work could be done by day except of course the usual necessary parades to keep the horses in condition & all the important work was carried out by night. Practically every night for the next fortnight all ranks were busy working up the establishment of Ammunition to the Battery positions. After the commencement of the Battle various small dumps were formed from which the Batteries were fed & the last of these was at GOUZEAUCOURT near the original front line. It was at this dump when the enemy counter attacked & captured GOUZEAUCOURT that a great number of the personnel of this Section were working and were captured. Most of them however did not give up the ghost but, when the Guards counter attacked during the day, they escaped from their Escorts & after an absence of 24 hours they trickled back to the Section by ones & two's very proud of their experiences. The Batteries continued in action in the open near GOUZEAUCOURT WOOD and owing to the advance made by the Huns all Ammunition had to be supplied from Woolwich Dump by Limbers. The work therefore continued to be very strenuous owing to the large expenditure of ammunition. Finally the Section with the Divisional Artillery was pulled out of action a few days before Christmas. The Section along with the R.A then entered on one of its most exciting and difficult marches. With the Horses & men fatigued & tired through endless hard work it had to face roads covered with snow & frozen making them like glass. The cold was intense & it was remarkable that so few accidents occurred. The weather continued to be severe & the roads in the same condition until the Artillery reached it old battle ground again the Ypres Salient; the batteries going into action on the right of the Menin Road & were supplied by Decauville. This Section was camped at Reninghelst and except for numerous fatigues, had a fairly easy time enabling men & horses to recover from their strenuous times in the past. There was no excitement while in this Sector & eventually the Divisional Artillery in February 1918 converged on Steenwerck & there entrained, their destination being NESLE & there took up rest billets and became G.H.Q reserve together with the rest of the Division. The Section was in billets in Rouy le Petit for about 6 weeks prior to the 21st of March 1918 in which time it had a splendid opportunity of getting

9

its personnel, horses & equipment in first class condition. On the 21st of March 1918, the first day of the great German Offensive, the 92 Bde to which this Section was attached received orders to move up & eventually came into action in the vicinity of Bray St Christophe, the Section and Battery Wagon Lines being encamped in Aubigny where a large Ammunition Dump had been established by the 30th Divisional Artillery. Very hard work commenced at once & during the night & the next day heavy Indents for Ammunition had to be fulfilled the work entailed being made more difficult owing to the frequent moves of the Batteries. Eventually the Batteries retired almost on to the Dump itself & the Section together with the Battery Wagon Lines were lying in the vicinity of Villers St Christophe with its Echelons full. On the following evening the Section was retiring via the Offoy Bridge when about 8 pm orders were received from O.C. 92 Bde that the Batteries would retire via Ham & that the Section should lie up between Villers St Christophe & Ham. About midnight heavy machine gun fire was noted on the ridge near Aubigny & Pip Squeaks landed in the Section's Lines & the position became rather uncertain. Orders were therefore given to prepare to retire & the Section then moved down towards Ham & halted. Reconnaissance was made into Ham to gain information and General Duncan who was then collecting the remainder of the 20th Machine Gunners was met & he said that the Germans might be expected in Ham at any time & that we were to move over the Ham Bridge at once & take the tired Machine Gunners on our Limbers as far as possible in the direction of Offoy Bridge which they were to defend. Fortunately the Section got clear of Ham without any incident except that on the other side of the Bridge difficulty was experienced owing to the darkness in squeezing the vehicles past a huge shellhole which was in the middle of the road. Everything came through however without a mishap but there is very little doubt that the heavy transport passing over the cobbled streets gave the Huns the clue that the last of the transport was passing through Ham & he immediately shelled the place very heavily. Apparently the 92 Bde had retired via Offoy during the night but it was not at all clear as to where it would come into action. The Section therefore retired via Esmery - Hallon & got in touch with the Brigade again before it came into action. The first halt was made at Solenté which was reached about midday and an Ammunition Dump was immediately formed and frequent journeys to & from the Batteries who were in action in the vicinity of Erchu were made during the remainder of the day & night. The following day further orders to retire were received & the Section established another Dump between Solente & Roiglise & on the next day orders were received that the Batteries were retiring & the Section moved back towards Roye where it encamped until about midnight when it became quite apparent that the enemy was pushing on with considerable speed. The Section therefore made a further move & marched during the whole night through Roye & halted to water & feed for an hour or so at Beuvraignes & then continued the retirement: the batteries being just in the rear. It marched during the greater part of the morning via Tilloy & finally halted at Gruvesnes about midday; horses & men being very fatigued & received a few hours welcome rest as the Batteries had not as yet come into action. Towards evening a further move was made & the Section then bivouaced in the open in the neighbourhood of Faverolles & stopped the night. That night the Batteries went into action & were supplied by the Section from a Corps Ammunition Dump between Faverolles & Montdidier. About 4 o'clock the following morning a further retirement was necessitated through Montdidier & advantage was taken to water the horses in the river Les 3 Sams. During that day the Section was supplying Ammunition & about 6 oclock in the evening it received orders to march North at once to Mailly Raineval. This was done during the night by making a splendid forced march arriving in the early hours of the morning. The Section bivouaced in this village during the day but the Batteries which were to have come into action at Braches did not do so. Having no Ammunition to supply that day the Section had a well earned rest until the following afternoon when a further retirement had to be made to Ailly sur-Noye which it reached in pouring rain & darkness late at night. The next day the Section again got in touch with the 92 Bde. who came into action on the east of ROUVREL. The next move was to Estrees-sur-Noye where a fairly large Ammunition Dump was made & the Batteries fed therefrom for several days. On the 4th day of April 1918 eventually the Section marched out & rejoined the Divisional Artillery which went into rest in the Abbeville area. About 12 days were spent cleaning up & reequipping and on the 16th of April the Divisional Artillery was ordered to march to Amiens a distance of about 30 miles which it did in one day. The following day it went into action the Batteries west of Villers-Brettonneux & this Section on the east side of Glissy. During the following days work was continuous night & day, the expenditure of Ammunition in this great Battle being very heavy indeed. After the elapse of about 12 days & the Huns had been stopped the Divisional Artillery were on the 28" April withdrawn and it marched on to the Lens front where it spent a quiet summer, this Section being at Gouy Servins. It was not until 9th October that the Divisional Artillery left the Lens front & marched to Arras & then to Cambrai & eventually on the 3rd of November came into action at Maresches the Section then being at Sommaing where there was an Ammunition Dump. A good deal of Ammunition was shot off in this advance & the difficulties experienced were made greater than otherwise would have been the case owing to the communications being daily lengthened as the enemy retired. On the 11" of November when hostilities ceased the Section was encamped at Breaugies near Bavay & had supplied the Batteries at Taisnieres.

When the Division came back to its Demobilization Area this Section established itself at Pommier where it built stabling & made things comfortable for the men, this work being completed a few days before Christmas after which demobilization started.

The foregoing is a brief account of the most notable performance of the Section while in France which it is hoped will convey to the reader some idea of the difficult & strenuous work that has been carried out in connection with the supply of Ammunition. It is only now desired to emphasize the fact that the Section is to be congratulated on its splendid good luck throughout the campaign – Considering the risks from Barrages put down by the enemy on Roads etc. leading up to the Batteries and the large target that Wagons & Horses make when trickling up to the advanced positions it is surprising that casualties have been so rare. Moreover when it is remembered that most of the work had been carried out at night often under intense shell fire & also the terrible nature of the Roads & Tracks that had to be traversed in all weathers in order to deliver the "stuff" that was so necessary to keep the guns in action the part played by all the Drivers & other Ranks of the Section cannot be too highly commended. Only those whose lot it has been to assist in carrying out this highly important work can realize how splendidly all Ranks in the Section have played the game.

In conclusion it is desired to mention that the Section has not only excelled at work but also at Sport. Its Football Team had a record which must have compared very favourably with any Team in the Division its Football always being of a very high order. At Cricket it could also put a Team in the field which could give most sides a very good game. Finally all Ranks in the Section will remember Xmas Day 1918 when the cessation of Hostilities was celebrated in a very fitting manner.

Roll of Honour.

Nº 70094,	Bombr	Plunkett J.	
57531	Bombr	Gliddon J.G.	
61896	L/Bdr	Hudson C.	
101144	Driver	Foster G	(Died)
43660	"	Phillips W	
114101	"	Zatkin F N	
97520	S.S.	Baker E	(Died)

Honours & Awards.

	Capt	T.A.	GULLIVER	M.C.
	Lieut	E.W.	AUSTIN	M.C.
61896,	Sgt	W.	ORR	M.M.
57412	"	E.	TOOKE	M.M.
69881	Bombr	W.	WHITE	M.M.

History of
No. 2 Section
20" B.A.C.

March 1909

History of 3rd Section 20th D.A.C.

Formation

We were formed as a Service unit for overseas in April 1915 under the command of Capt. Henderson R.F.A. Our training until we embarked for overseas was interesting; also trying at times on account of our mules being fresh and untrained for that purpose of which they were needed.

Arrival in France

We entrained at Larkhill on the 22nd of July 1915 after considerable difficulty with the animals. Arriving at Southampton we embarked without difficulty whatever, reaching Le Havre on the night of the 23rd. Disembarkation was carried out on the morning of the 24th, were entrained and proceeded to Lombres the same day. Again we met with trouble while unloading the animals, one mule killing itself on the ramp. We then marched to our first billets in France, which did not come up to our expectations, tired and somewhat fed up as we all were.

First time in Action

About the middle of August we went into action for the first time at Fleurbaix and our surprise was great to find things so quiet. Our time here was easy, until our first real engagement in the battle of Loos on the 21st September, when we began to realize there was a war on. We were kept very busy at all times night and day running ammunition up to the guns. At this period ammunition was difficult to obtain, sometimes waiting twelve to fourteen hours at the Corps dump for it to arrive.

Changing our Front.

After Loos nothing of importance happened, excepting that we lost our O.C. Capt Henderson who was replaced by Capt. Laing. January 1916 we moved from this sector under sealed orders, and finished up at Poperinghe on the Ypres front, being our second time in Action. Our realizations of war was again confirmed on this front it being somewhat warmer than the last. Here we gained the first honour for the Section.

First Award

No   Cpl Coveney. G. was awarded the D.C.M. for bravery at Brelin. He was detached from the unit and attached to the 92nd Brigade R.F.A. H.Q. for wire laying in the forward area. A bombardment was expected and the area to be straffed could only be observed from one O.P. Cpl Coveney repaired lines under very heavy shell fire from the enemy. Finally the lines were rendered useless and he ran a fresh wire from the guns

2

to the O.P. This brave act kept communications intact and the bombardment was carried out successfully.

Rest

After three months here in action we went to rest at Roubrouck, where keen competition arose with units for smartness and cleanliness with men animals harness wagons etc. Competition was so great in the Division that a Horse Show was organized to display our abilities at Zeggars Cappel in April when this Section took 1st and 3rd prize for the best turned out teams in the D.A.C.

Reorganization

At Roubrouck the D.A.C. was reorganized, this Section becoming No 4 Section and the largest in the D.A.C. This altered our work somewhat in the fact that hereafter our chief work was running R.E. material to the line for use in the trenches.

Casualties

Our first casualties occurred at Menin Gate R.E. Dump where two drivers (one seriously & one slightly) were wounded, also four mules.

March to the Somme

In September we prepared to march to the Somme. We were congratulated on this march for being up to this time the best turned out unit seen in France by General Sir H. Plumer. Previous to this march we sent an advance Section to the Somme in July, the work rendered by this advance Section to our Infantry at the battle Guillemont, was considered of great importance. Entirely working with the Infantry for all purposes.

At Guillemont

During this battle our wagons and limbers appeared to look gruesome for they were smothered with blood from carrying wounded, both our own and hostile, from the First Aid Posts to the dressing stations.

Good bye to the Somme

After nine months tedious but uneventful work on the Somme, we marched again to the Ypres Sector and here met with the blackest period of our time in France. We were panzed in for the battle of Pilkim Ridge and Langemarck. Here were had

Casualties

casualties almost daily. Our biggest casualties occurred on the night of 23rd July 1917 whilst running ammunition to 91st Bdge R.F.A. guns, we had three killed and six wounded and a great number of animals were lost. About this time we sent another advance Section to Elverdinghe, which had a very

3

firing time, supplying the Infantry with S.A.A. bombs etc, carried by pack mules for the battle of Langemarck. During this period we had two more awards Dr Lythgoe gaining the M.M. for rescuing wounded from Gas, this act being difficult for the driver as he was in charge of a six mule team, which he had to abandon for a time, and he eventually being the wagon and team safely back to camp on his own. Bdr Tatchell. A. No   was also awarded the M.M. for conspicuous work during a firing of ammunition by enemy shell fire.

Back to the Somme and Cambrai

We were released from this front in September and entrained at Proven for the Somme again. Things were fairly quiet here for a time until Nov 20th when we advance on Cambrai. Here again we sent advance Sections to each Infantry Brigades with pack animals to follow up the advance with rations and ammunition. About this time the D.A.C was reorganized No 3 Section becoming the SAA Section and worked practically entirely with the Div Infantry. At this time we lost our O.C. Capt W Laing who went as Major to command a Battery. Capt A.J.J. McDonald then took over.

Back to Ypres

Wind up again, back to the Ypres Sector. Here things did not come up to our expectations, we found things rather quiet much to our surprise, having been to Ypres before. Nothing remarkable happened to us here.

Another Rest

On 17.2.18 we left Ypres for the last time, and the old boys left of the Section thanked the Gods for their deliverance from this Sector. We entrained at Steenbeck for Nesle, marched to Rouy le Petit for the rest which was greatly needed. Here we had three weeks good rest whilst preparing for the March Offensive.

March Offensive

On March 21st we had a hurried move forward. Fritz was expected and we were called on again for that work which we had previously been praised for. Throughout the twelve days of retirement this Section upheld its reputation by never failing to supply its Infantry with SAA, bombs, Grenades etc. Two more awards were gained here. No   Cpl Williams A and No   Bdr Harpman M earned the M.M. for keeping up a ceaseless supply of ammunition to our Infantry at great personal risk.

Not broken but badly bent.

We came out of action on the 1-4-18 owing to the Division being in such a deplorable state, and went

3.

to Longroy for a short rest, and refitted which was badly needed at that time. Taking to the road once more we moved up to the Lens section where we were in action until October. Nothing startling happened here and on the whole had a fairly easy and quiet time, excepting that we lost our O.C. Capt. McDonald who went to England on leave and never returned owing to sickness. He was replaced by our present O.C. Capt. A.T. Gulliver M.C. R.F.A.

The Corps Horse Show. Whilst in action on this front the 8th Corps Horse Show was arranged. We competed two teams which was approved by the Divisional Horse Show that was held for the purpose of selecting entries for the Division at the Corps Show. Our two teams gained the Red and Blue rosettes from Division but were knocked out in the Corps Show.

After Fritz. We left Lens in October and marched to Cambligneul, where we had a short rest. Entraining at Savy we were congratulated by the Divl. General for being the quickest unit to entrain, the time being 32 minutes. The R.T.O. at this Station said that he had never seen in his experience this operation carried out in such an orderly way. We detrained at Frémicourt and marched to Cambrai in great spirits, knowing Fritz was on the run. The excitement was not what we expected, Fritz was going fast, and we were expecting to be banged into action, but were held in reserve until such times as the Armistice was signed, which was overwhelming for us who had spent 3½ years in our opinion, good work to our Division.

Epilogue Our trying times over, we await demobilization in the peaceful French village of Warlincourt-Le-Pas, where visions of Blighty and England are ever with us. We are very thankful for our deliverance from the strafe, those that are left of us. Our comrades who have fallen will always hold a warm spot in the annals of No 3 Section 20th D.A.C. R.F.A.

A.T. Gulliver Capt R.F.A.
Comdg No 3 Section 20 D.A.C.